THE MALADY AND THE REMEDY

AN INTERNATIONAL ESSAY ANTHOLOGY ON HUMAN RIGHTS ABUSE IN AFRICA

A PUBLICATION OF THE INTERNATIONAL HUMAN RIGHTS
ART FESTIVAL (IHRAF)
AFRICAN CHAPTER

THE MALADY AND THE REMEDY
Copyright @ 2021
International Human Rights Art Festival (IHRAF)
E-mail: ihrafnigeria@gmail.com, woleadedoyin@gmail.com.
Tel: +234(0)8072673852

First Published 2021

Design by Michele Chu
Cover photo by Eelco Bohtlingk/Unsplash

CONTENTS

EDITOR'S NOTE

"Activism works. So what I'm telling you to do now is to act, because no one is too small to make a difference."

It is line with and in response to the above witty saying by Greta Thunberg, a Swedish activist and Amnesty International Ambassador of Conscience, that this masterpiece has stormed the literary world, to question and quench the issues of human rights abuses and violations in Africa.

A collection of twenty essays, this anthology was birthed out of mutual quest by some concerned and ardent minds, who are interested and are determined to make a difference in the 'stories' of human rights in Africa, and, in fact, in the world at large. These humans were committed to rooting out the noxious and lethal malady called 'Human Right Abuse' which has eaten deep into the root, the soul, the freedom and the general existence of humanity, both in Africa and in the entire world in general.

This ardency was first registered, when, in March 2021, the African Chapter of the International Human Rights Art Festival (IHRAF), headed by Wole Adedoyin, made a call for submission, seeking for essays from writers in Africa, on human rights abuse and violation in the continent and beyond.

This initiative and the 'call for submissions' were not only focused on positively 're-writing the stories' and bettering the situation of human rights in Africa; it also assembled some benefits for the subscribers, by ways of certification, honourable mention, and publication. The call also came with prizes mapped for the authors of the best three essays, which were endowed in honour of some Africa human rights heroes and activists, as follows: Nelson Mandela Prize—1st prize, Thomas Sankara Prize—2nd prize, and Omoyele Sowore Prize—3rd prize.

In response to this call, forty-five essays were received from writers from different African countries, which are all thematic, responsive, and efficacious, with regards to the rules of the Call and purpose of the initiative.

Independently judged by Nigerian author and journalist, Izunna Okafor, and American author, artist and playwright, Tom Block, twenty of these essays were longlisted based on specific criteria, out of which thirteen were further shortlisted (still on based specific criteria); while three were meritoriously declared winners (also on specific criteria). There were also some honourable mentions. These three essays and essayists adjudged winners and awarded the respective prizes earlier mentioned are: ***"Human Rights Abuse and Violations in Africa: It's a Crime to be Happy in My Country"*** (by Ugochukwu Anadi)—1st prize; ***"Teenage Sexual Molestation: Rethinking the Havoc on the Girl Child"*** (by Charles Iornumbe)—2nd prize; and ***"Human Rights Abuse and Violations in Africa: Gross Domestic Violence Against Women"*** (by Osho Tunde)—3rd prize.

Following the awarding of these promised cash prizes to their respective winners, and with the 'honourable mention' and 'certification' promises also fulfilled, the next promised item that apparently remain is the 'publication' promise; and that is what this anthology has come to fulfil.

Although only the shortlisted essays and essayists were promised publication during the 'call for submissions', it became really wise to adjust further to accommodate all the longlisted essays and essayists in this publication, beholding the perceived extraordinary quality, relevance and efficacy of their contents in actualising the overall goal of the initiative, which is to promote human rights values in Africa and positively influence the betterment of the human rights situation in the continent.

It is the conglomeration, editing and publication of these twenty longlisted essays that gave birth to this classic anthology, entitled **"The Malady and the Remedy"**.

The essays published herein take both the form of stories/narratives, analyses, etc, to x-ray, bemoan, condemn and challenge the incessant abuse and violation of human rights in Africa, the unsafeness of Africa for human rights activists and freedom fighters, as well as recommend the elixirs to all these ills against humanity.

Aside its intriguing, thought-provoking, informative, educative and didactic qualities, another most outstanding feature of this anthology is that the essays published therein do not just condemn human rights violations and make recommendations; they are research-based and deep-rooted. In other words, these essays experientially and comparably look deep into the history of human rights and human rights abuse/violation in Africa, the causes, the types, what and what have been done so far to better the situation, why those things are not yielding the expected results, and finally propose/present better and more efficacious alternatives to addressing this age-long issue of human rights abuse, borrowing from the experience of yesterday, the situation of today, and the projection for tomorrow.

Indeed, this anthology is a must-read for everyone who loves human rights and freedom. Every human being deserves to be treated as a human, for his being. Freedom fighting and right activism should be for all and for everyone. Human rights are for every human; and Africans are humans. For every other thing regarding that, flip through the pages of this anthology, and come out a better activist.

Izunna Okafor
The Editor
+234(0)8163938812
Izunnaokafor70@gmail.com

WOMEN'S INALIENABLE RIGHT TO RESPECTFUL MATERNITY CARE

BETTY IGE

Three days after a painful childbirth, Emma Kadri started experiencing vaginal inflammation. Following a visit to the University Teaching Hospital in her city, long hours and a surgical procedure, a traumatized Emma was discharged after two uncomfortable nights in a crowded female ward. What happened to the young woman who should have been at home enjoying the pleasures of motherhood? During her short stay in the hospital, Emma had confided in Dr. Gbemi, a medical director. According to Emma, the midwife at the Community Health Centre had roughly stitched her torn vagina, all the time slapping her thighs and subjecting her to verbal abuse.

Abuses in different forms exist in every part of the world. For example, in an article titled 'Human Rights Violations', Amnesty International's 2009 World Report and other studies show that individuals are tortured or abused in at least 81 countries; face unfair trials in at least 54 countries; restricted in their freedom of expression in at least 77 countries. Not only that, but women and children in particular are marginalized in numerous ways; the press is not free in many countries, and dissenters are silenced, too often permanently. Violation of human right is not peculiar to any specific people or situation. It can happen to anyone, in any place, at any time, and in any life situation. The problem continues to plague Africa today and vulnerable groups such as women and children are not excluded, as can be seen in the story of Emma Kadri.

Human rights violation is a common but complex phenomenon. It is seen as a destructive and disruptive practice. Indeed, the majority of research and information in the human rights field is predicated on this fact. One of the most challenging aspects of human rights violations is in defining the scope of the problem. This is because of alleged cover-ups and denials associated with the issue. Truth be told, in every society there are conditions that support the promotion of peace. It starts with the inviolability of fundamental human rights. Too often conflicts arise because human rights are infringed on. And when the right of the human person is disrespected, it creates disharmony which in turn tears the fabric of peaceful coexistence that holds the society together.

The concept of human right should not be a mere theoretical notion. From the creation viewpoint, the existence of humankind is accompanied by fundamental and inalienable rights. A person is inherently entitled to these rights simply because he or she is a created human being.

Any attempt to breach or violate these rights without justification becomes an abuse of fundamental human right. Hence, this paper takes a gender perspective to examine the problem of human rights violation against women who need reproductive healthcare services.

Mistreatment of women during childbirth is a menace. Women worldwide are confronted with this problem, not only in poorer countries but also within developed countries. No wonder many case studies, formal and informal discussions, and information on maternal mortality and morbidity have identified healthcare providers' mistreatment of women during childbirth as a critical barrier to reducing maternal deaths across the globe. In fact, evidence generated through the Human Reproductive Program's (HRP) Alliance research capacity strengthening program suggests that this unacceptable mistreatment of women can include physical and verbal abuse, violations of privacy, stigma and discrimination, and neglect and abandonment. Other forms of human rights abuse and violation include painful vaginal examination, pinching, slapping, yelling, poor physical conditions of labour rooms/facility, and physical restraint to a delivery bed.

Further, numerous studies have revealed that many African countries refuse women access to respectful healthcare and deprive them of the ability to make their own reproductive health choices. Situations in Africa where health workers are insensitive to the plight of pregnant women and attend to them with wrong attitudes abound. For example, Mamadou Dioulde Balde et al. in their article titled 'Perceptions and Experiences of the Mistreatment of Women during Childbirth in Health Facilities in Guinea: A Qualitative Study with Women and Service Providers' reveal that anecdotal reports from women and healthcare providers in Guinea suggest that women may be mistreated during childbirth, such as being pinched, slapped, and verbally abused.

Improving how women are treated during childbirth is a non-negotiable basic right of every African woman irrespective of her social background or economic class. It is imperative that substantial progress be made to discourage abuse and disrespect meted on women during the delivery process. This is because inadequate quality and respectful reproductive health services constitutes human rights abuse. This worrisome trend has been linked to an estimated 300,000 maternal deaths that occur per year in developing countries from complications during pregnancy and childbirth.

Respectful healthcare must be given to women during childbirth to safeguard the mental health of women and to prevent abuse and avoidable deaths of mothers and babies. A proper implementation of the human rights norms and standards is a core function necessary to deal with human rights issues and serve the needs of African citizens. Advocacy for a human rights culture which focuses on respectful and dignified maternity care during childbirth should not only recognize the achievement of sustainable development goals but should also maintain a progressive African human rights jurisprudence by recommending appropriate punishment for health workers who violate women's right to respectful maternity care. More so, reproductive care policies should include recommendations for adequate training of compassionate and skilled birth attendants/midwives; provision of quality healthcare services and systems; reduced cost of healthcare; increased motivation of health workers in terms of pay and skills advancement; and improved sensitization of women and healthcare givers during antenatal and postnatal visits.

Human rights are the basic rights and freedoms that belong to every person in the world, from birth until death regardless of race, sex, nationality, ethnicity, language, religion, or any other status. Hence, despite the complexity of human rights violations, it is worth noting that adequate human rights education is a potent tool policymakers can use to curtail abuses especially against vulnerable groups such as women and children in African societies. In essence, every childbearing woman in Africa has the inalienable right to respect, dignity, privacy, freedom to express her concern and make informed choices concerning her reproductive health.

BETTY IGE, *whose works are published locally and internationally in various journals, magazines, and anthologies, is the author of Clockwise, a chapbook of poetry. A writer, social entrepreneur, and bibliophile, her mission is to promote the reading culture and make reading a commonplace experience.*

IT'S A CRIME TO BE HAPPY IN MY COUNTRY

UGOCHUKWU ANADỊ

When people hear that it's a crime to be happy in my country, they cringe, and look at me with a face that screams disbelief. They do not understand how it can be a crime to be happy in any part of the world, not to talk more of a country like the so-called Giant of Africa, which one sometime saw itself amongst the list of countries with the happiest citizens. And the disbelief is justified; one cannot argue that it's a crime to be happy in a country that has more comedians than citizens. So, what makes me say so?

I first saw the word *gay* in a novel, the name of which I cannot remember. It was used to describe the mood of a poor intelligent Nigerian secondary school graduate whose intelligence fetched a full scholarship to study outside the country. The young secondary school graduate who I'll call Ike for the purpose of this work had borrowed heavily to write the examination which would make him, without any financial burden, a Mechanical Engineering student of Harvard University upon passing. The author made us know that when Ike received the letter that stated that he passed the examination, he jumped up and ran round his family's compound, waving the letter, like a patriotic citizen would do the flag of his newly independent country. The author concluded that he was in a *gay mood*.

Further readings as I grew, taught me that being gay is a positive adjective; that it's an adjective used to describe things like when one is *happily excited*, or *keenly alive* and *exuberant*, or when something is *bright* and *lively*. To be gay was something my young mind always aspired to, and most often than not an aspiration that gets real for me, living under so wonderful and religious a parent. So I was confused and at the same time shocked, when in Jan 2014, a law which caused uproar in the country was passed. This law which received lots of applause from my religious circle (my parents inclusive) I later learnt was called, *The Same-Sex Prohibition Law*. But before learning the name of this controversial law, I already knew it as the *anti-gay law*.

The boy who at an early age of readership had known being gay as being happy, is now told that being gay is a crime that can lead him, or any other Nigerian, to some fourteen years behind the iron bars of the Nigerian Correctional Centres. I mean, the boy just discovered that to be happy is to be a criminal in his country.

While it's now evident to me that my confusion and shock was out of a semantic insufficiency (being a boy who grew in a typical Nigerian religious family where the topic of sex and human sexuality is only mumbled about, as if it's an evil spirit one dares not call out aloud), the submission that being happy in my country is a crime still holds.

To be gay is: to love, to admire, to bound, to strive for companionship, in just the same way a non-gay person would, the difference in this case being the sex of the companion. While the non-gay person finds this companionship and love in a person who possesses different sex organs from him, the gay person, just like wires, will get this attraction if their currents (their sex) are moving in the same direction. To deny a gay person this right to love and live, to be himself or herself, to be in a caring companionship and relationship is simply to deny the gay person a right to be happy. It's simply to say to such a person that he should be contented with just existing, that he should never strive to live, that his happiness is a threat to the state and therefore a crime. That he can never dare to be happy.

And for many centuries, this has been the lot of the gay person in Nigeria, and many other African countries. The happiness of a gay person in Africa is a crime that's being punished by many years of imprisonment; and even in some countries, a capital punishment, which we had failed to stipulate for our rulers who in their corrupt practices have continued to make us lesser humans.

To end the story of Ike, different from how the author did, Ike in that gay mood, after showing the letter to his parents and siblings, rushed towards the gate and was soon seen raising the dust along the pathway that led to Amadi's house. Amadi, who everyone in the village knew to be Ike's best friend, was a classmate of Ike who lived a few houses away from Ike. Amadi and Ike were always found together: doing their assignments, going to the church, going to the community's secondary school (their school), going to the stream to fetch water everywhere like newly wedded couples. Theirs was the perfect example of a good friendship as far as parents in their little, yet to be developed neighbourhood are concerned. Theirs was a friendship between two serious and dedicated students of a high moral standing, who never allowed girls to come in between their studies like most of their mates did. In fact, as far as Ike and Amadi are involved, girls, no matter how beautiful they are, do not exist. Sexual promiscuity is a word that shouldn't have been in the dictionary.

So one can imagine the shock on Amadi's mothers face, when

she opened the door to Amadi's small room having returned from the market and not seeing him around and found the two boys in each other's arms, lips glued, tongues entwined. It was to her as if she had seen the devil himself, and never knew when the scream left her mouth. It was the scream that brought the two friends and lovers back to the room, same scream that brought the neighbours into the compound. Amadi and Ike had to suffer discrimination amongst their peers from that day henceforth, the two best kids in the neighbourhood became the worst kids, giving the other boys who had been told to emulate the two friends and abandon their promiscuous life a field day. The parents of the two kids believed that it was the handwork of their enemies; that it was some demonic manipulations, and thus sent their kids to their pastor for a deliverance session. Ike never survived the canes and hunger he was subjected to in the name of deliverance, and an emotionally shattered Amadi later joined his friend through the veins he set free from his wrist. And like that, two promising young men were lost.

The human rights abuses and violations going on against gay people in our society have robbed us and continue to rob us of many talented members of the society. It has made many of those we claim to love, those we claim to want to make their lives better, go into hiding; burying themselves in their bodies and making the closet their only succour. It has made many unscrupulous security agents to kill, maim and extort suspected gay people without any fear; for they know that nobody will speak for these people, who even the nation's law is against their existence. It has driven many of our youths to their self-prepared graves and many others beyond the shores of our seas. It has injected the virus called hate in the minds of our kids. And one thing this virus does is that it permeates every aspect of our communal existence without our knowledge and poisons them because hate anywhere is hate everywhere. It divides us into 'us' and 'them' (gays and non-gays) and makes it impossible for us to appreciate differences and diversities in our society.

Our religious leaders who preach love and peace should be the leaders in the fight against this virus called hate. Our educational institutes should teach that any form of happiness that does not in any way threaten the existence of our specie should never be a crime; and the government should make sure that her citizens are happy.

We cannot continue to abuse the rights of our citizens; we cannot continue to deny and deprive people of their happiness, just because they are in the minority and expect our countries, our mother Africa to progress. We must come together and say with one voice that there's nothing corrective about corrective rapes, that the security agents have no business bursting into people's room if what's going on in that room is not a threat to the society and state; and that there's nothing converting about conversion therapies. We must come together and make laws to protect the vulnerable amongst us, but above all, we must educate our people to rise above hate and prejudice, for a better Africa.

UGOCHUKWU ANADỊ *is a 20-year old student of the University of Nigeria, Nsukka. He hails from Neni in Anaocha Local Government Area of Anambra State.*

HUMAN RIGHTS ABUSE AND VIOLATIONS IN AFRICA

SAMUEL EPHRAIM EDWARD

After about three hundred centuries of slavery which was succeeded by a ravaging wind of colonialism and imperialism, Africa has remained a fertile ground for gross human rights violations. Regrettably, the socio-political landscape of the continent is fraught with a litany of heinous acts of man's inhumanity to man perpetuated with the machinery of government. From Egypt to Kenya to Burkina Faso to Mali to mention but a few, police brutality, extrajudicial killings and arbitrary use of force against civilians have defied existing initiatives. This begs the question: When would Africa ever have enough of her woes?

Historically, the repressive apartheid regime in South Africa had remained the most prominent institutionalized avenue of human rights violation. Yet, even with many decades having passed by, the monster has remained a thorn in the flesh of citizenship in different countries of the continent. Unlike what defined apartheid, human rights infringement in Africa is now a case of "Dog eating dog; blacks against black". However, for the purpose of this work, the state of human rights and its violations in the Nigerian context will be made the focal point, reason being that experiences shared are from a more familiar terrain.

Back in 1995 during the military regime of General Sani Abacha, international eyebrows were raised when nine Ogoni elders including Ken Saro Wiwa were gruesomely executed by the then military government. What crime did they commit? They spoke up against the deplorable environmental condition of the Ogoni Land occasioned by the activities of oil companies operating in the area—same issue that has remained a cause for concern up till today in the Niger Delta region. That the military regime of General Sani Abacha sanctioned the killings of those statesmen without due trial demonstrated the level of impunity, and this proved costly, as many nations and international bodies broke diplomatic ties with Nigeria.

Granted it could be excusable that sanity was thrown to pigs when referring to the Ogoni Killing that the execution happened in a military regime, but it defies every sense of decorum and civility to recall not to talk of admitting that the government under a democratic dispensation in 1999 could order the military to ransack a small town called Odi in Bayelsa State, killing scores of civilians in a reprisal attack for an alleged attack on military officers in the town. In the same vein, if it could be reasonably contented that the Odi Killings happened when Nigeria's democracy was still at its infant stage in 1999, how then would one explain that a repeat of such mindless employ of state's force against its own citizen by government could be made a topic in 2020?

Undoubtedly, an integral part of every democratic set-up is peaceful demonstration in the form of protests. This is even provided for in the Nigerian Constitution of 1999 as amended. To say that the nationwide #ENDSARS protest by young but socially conscious Nigerians in October 2020 against police brutality and extrajudicial killings which eventually snowballed into calls for an end to bad governance in the country resulted in a massacre is inconceivable.

20th October 2020 will go down as the day Nigerian government through men and officers of the Nigerian Army opened fire and killed scores of peaceful protesters at Lekki Tollgate in Lagos. This rings bells of the least importance placed on right to life in the Africa's most populous country. Following the unprovoked massacre, Amnesty International reported on 21st October 2020 that not less than 12 protesters were killed at the scene of the incident, a report the government and its mercenaries had done everything negatively doable to deny casualties or any incident of use of force, even with glaring evidences.

Very tellingly, with Nigeria being signatories to many international treaties which promote the sanctity of human life both on the African scene and on the international arena, it would be ordinarily expected that the dignity of the human person would be treated with utmost sacredness. The African Charter on Human and People's Rights which came into effect in 1986 and the Convention against Torture and Other Cruel Inhuman or Degrading Treatments are examples of treaties which have been signed and ratified by Nigeria. This is in addition to the country's signature and ratification of the Covenant on Civil and Political Rights (ICCPR), which emphasizes the legal obligation binding on Nigeria to protect human rights within the territorial confines of the country as reiterated in section 33(1) of the 1999 Constitution.

Apart from the near non-existent nature of human rights in the form of use of military force against civilians, forced evictions from places of residence without genuine consultation and adequate notice, compensation or alternative accommodation constitute gross human rights violation. Having been a victim of forceful eviction without any prior notification or compensation sometime in 2014, I can say it is a terrible experience. The officials of my local government had ensured I became a destitute with no roof under my head for as long as I could seek shelter elsewhere.

Moreover, regular intimidation and harassment of human rights defenders and journalists have been made a culture now in the scheme of things in Nigeria. It is even surprising for an activist not to have a prison experience in the course of the discharge of his duties. This is a scenario one of Nigeria's finest human rights defender, Omoloye Sowore couldn't outdo as he was made to spend "quality time" in the custody of the State Security Service for daring to speak up against monumental ineptitude in the art of governance through his "Revolution Now" initiative. His detention in custody even defied court orders that sanctioned his release. But the powers that be had promised to "show him pepper". Sowore's case is just one out of the many unreported acts of intimidation faced by human rights activists and journalists.

More so, press freedom in Nigeria is still doubtful as freedom of speech is permitted but "freedom after speech" is not guaranteed. Nigeria is still far from achieving that level of freedom of press that is commensurate with the over 21 years of democratic experience in which the country shamelessly boast of. In April 2020, Reporters without Borders ranked Nigeria 115 out 180 in terms of countries with tested press freedom. With this report, one would be tempted to jump up in excitement because it is not as bad as this article has "painted it". The reason for the low ranking, as explained by the body, is because of the continued killings, detention and brutalization of journalists alongside targeted attempts to shrink the civic space by the government.

In the furtherance, another report by Transparency International within the same period had it that with over hundred independent newspapers operating in the country, Nigeria enjoys great media pluralism. But journalism bordering on politics, terrorism and financial impropriety could easily be tagged "Hate speech" with some very dire consequences to follow.

While it is difficult to resist the temptation of beaming the searchlight on the excesses of some unprofessional members of the Nigeria Police Force as well as the now disbanded Special Anti-Robbery Squad (SARS) who subject good-looking and seemingly "well-to-do" young Nigerians to undue scrutiny and unholy search because they appear so "sophisticated and comfortable for their age", the incessant roadblocks by security outfit who extort money from commuters equally constitute human rights violation.

By way of conclusion, a myriad of factors are responsible for the violation of human rights in the country. These are not unconnected to institutionalized impunity where human rights offenders go unpunished and are left off the hook, dysfunctional criminal justice system, godfatherism and politically motivated violations as well as endemic systematic corruption. These problems that abate human rights violations are man-made, which means that with the right political willpower coupled with some ethical re-orientation and attitudinal re-engineering, these ills can be undone for the better of human lives in Nigeria. It behoves on all and sundry to begin to feel that the limit has been reached and even exceeded; and so there is need for collective effort at ensuring that the narrative changes for the better, because when a chain stays longer than normal on the neck; it may be mistaken for jewellery.

SAMUEL EPHRAIM EDWARD *is a novelist and poet. His works are published in selected online literary journals. He lives in Uyo, Nigeria.*

GENERAL IDEA OF HUMAN RIGHTS ABUSE AND VIOLATION

PHILIP ONYIMOWO

Human rights are the basic rights and freedom that belong to every human being in the world from birth until death. The human rights are set of rights agreed upon by a community and given to every human being to ensure the protection of their dignity, freedom, status, humanity and justice and seek also to address specific problems such as; guaranteeing fair trials, ending slavery, ensuring availability of education etc. Human rights are claim rights that focus on the freedom, protection, status and benefit of the right holder (Beitz 2009). The Universal Declaration of Human Rights (UDHR) was proclaimed by the United Nations General Assembly in Paris on 10th December, 1948 (General Assembly Resolution 217A). The recognition of the inalienable rights of all members of the human family is the basis for the human rights declaration, as these rights are recognised as the foundation of peace, freedom, justice and equality in the world. Human rights seek to create a world of balance, justice and freedom for everyone irrespective of race, gender, colour, caste, religion and economic class.

In Africa, there has been a great contempt and disregard for the basic rights of humans which has led to the abuse of human rights in Africa. Human rights abuse and violation occur when actions by state and non-state ignore or deny an individuals their basic human rights. The violated rights can include civil, political, cultural, social, religious and economic rights. To violate or abuse a person's right is to deny that person of his/her fundamental moral entitlement and treat them as undeserving of respect and dignity. In Africa, the socially disadvantaged group of society which includes women, children, persons with disabilities, ethnic moralities and people living with poverty are more susceptible to the abuse and violation of their basic human rights.

EXAMPLES OF HUMAN RIGHTS ABUSE AND VIOLATION IN AFRICA
It is on record that during the global COVID-19 pandemic that hit the globe, human rights violation escalated in African countries. The pandemic recorded a high rate of racial injustice and police brutality while the internet shutdown violated the rights to life-saving information about the global health crisis. In Algeria, major human rights issues include unauthorised intrusion of privacy, restriction of freedom of the press, domestic violence against women, sexual abuse of LGBTI persons and human trafficking.

By April 2018, a UN document reported that thousands of horrible human rights violation had been performed by state affiliated militias in Libya. These groups carried out random attacks in densely populated areas leading to the death of over a thousand civilians.

By 2016 in Egypt, public criticism of the government was declared banned, thereby placing a restriction on the rights of freedom of expression. Also, the continued torture of detainees and their unaccounted mysterious disappearance were breach on their human rights.

On 12th-14th December 2015, the Nigerian Army carried

out a massacre of 347 members of Islamic Movement of Nigeria (IMN) in Zaria, Kaduna state. In March 2020, it was revealed that some Nigerian army officers took advantage of food shortage and abused women in exchange of granting them food. On 20th October 2020, End SARS protesters were massacred in great number by Military men at the Lekki Toll Gate in Lagos, Nigeria. In over 20 African countries, people were denied their rights to peaceful protest through unlawful bans, use of excessive force, harassment and arbitrary arrests.

Throughout the 1990s, African governments, one after the other, set up their own national human rights commission through support from the UN and international donors, but supporting statistics of cases of human rights abuse and violation in Africa reveal that despite the presence of organisations and agencies charged with the protection of human rights, human rights violation in Africa still persists at a highly increasing rate by instrument of state and non-state.

CAUSES OF HUMAN RIGHTS ABUSE AND VIOLATION IN AFRICA

The causes of human rights abuse and violation in Africa range from one geographical area to another. However, the leading causes of human rights abuse and violation in Africa include ignorance, political instability, racial discrimination, post-colonialism, economic scarcity, religious bigotry, lack of judicial autonomy and freedom of the press, restriction on the freedom of the press, lack or absence of independence and neutrality in the judiciary, debt and bad financial management, monopoly of power, unauthorized intrusion of privacy, establishment of law barring specific of free expression, corruption of government officials, actions of state and non-state as well as domestic violence.

SOLUTIONS TO HUMAN RIGHTS ABUSE AND VIOLATION IN AFRICA
For the purpose of this essay, two major solutions to human rights abuse and violation will be considered.

The first step to help prevent human rights abuse and violation in Africa is gaining adequate knowledge on human rights and equally knowing where to go and what to do to seek redress if your rights are violated. In Africa, the socially disadvantaged majority and people living with poverty should be given adequate education on their rights and how to seek justice when their basic human rights are violated. Human rights organizations and agencies should provide adequate information to the masses on their basic human rights and what to do when such rights are violated.

Secondly, judiciary independence and freedom of the press should be highly practiced. Most African societies practice Democracy; and in a system that practices Democracy, judicial independence and freedom of the press are of high importance to help conserve human rights. The judiciary should be able to decide matters before them impartially, on the basis of facts and in accordance with the law without fear or favour.

Courts should be granted absolute autonomy and should not be subject to improper influence and pressure from any other body either for private or partisan interest. When this happens, full confidence will be placed on the Justice process of the Judiciary. The marginalized majority and lower class of the society will also have full assurance that their cases of human right violation and abuse will be decided fairly and in accordance with the law.

Freedom of the press should also be ensured. According to article 19 of the United Nations Universal Declaration of Human Rights, "Everyone has the right to freedom of opinion and expression; this right includes freedom to hold opinions without interference and impart information and ideas through the media regardless of frontiers." The press should serve the governed and not only those in power. Freedom of expression of the individual and the media is a right that must be upheld in Democratic societies.

Human rights abuse and violation has come a long way and will continue to linger in the African society if adequate measures are not taken to ensure that every human being is treated worthy of justice, peace, freedom and dignity.

PHILIP ONYIMOWO *writes from Benue State, Nigeria.*

GROSS DOMESTIC VIOLENCE AGAINST WOMEN

OSHO TUNDE

Today, something deplorable is plaguing the world. The violations and abuse of human rights seem to remain a replayed song in Africa and many parts of the world. Defenceless people are daily being trampled upon by the powerful, and the heart of it all is the age-long domestic violence against women.

A one-time United Nations Secretary-General, Kofi Annan opined in 1999 that "Violence against women is perhaps the most shameful human rights violation."

Although, according to Koffi, it knows no boundaries of geography, culture or wealth, yet a United Nations report reveals that African women are most exposed to this domestic violence. In sub-Saharan Africa as a whole, 22.3% women aged 15-49 experience physical and sexual violence within a 12 month calendar. In Kenya, 2003 report of the Attorney General's office revealed 47% domestic violence of all homicide. Amnesty International reports in South Africa that about one woman is killed by her husband or boyfriend every six hours. The World Health Organization (WHO) in 2005 found out that 50% of women in Tanzania and 71% in Ethiopia are reportedly beaten. Reality asserts that at least one-third of African women are daily facing beatings, sexual harassments, rapes, forced marriages among others from their men counterparts who feel it is culturally expedient to do so.

Consequently, these violations and abuses bring about a growing incidence of trauma, physical damage and deaths among women in the continent. However, this paper contends that unless all the mechanisms safeguarding human rights and of course, women's rights in Africa, are strengthened for more effective exploit, violence against women and other gutless humans in Africa may know no end.

ROOTS OF DOMESTIC VIOLENCE

Its existence can be traced to a number of factors:

• *Colonial Background.* The colonialists' ideology of 'Domesticity', which Nigeria and some parts of Africa were persuaded to adopt in the early era of colonialists and Christian missionaries, reduced the esteemed position of women to mere sexual activities, trading, field labour, baby weaning and meal preparations. No wonder, out of 25 secondary schools established in 1920, 3 were girls only and a whole 22 were exclusively for boys.

The 1922 Clifford Constitution under indirect rule prevented women from voting. In 1929, about 50 women in Aba, Nigeria were murdered in cold blood for speaking up against the violation of their socioeconomic rights. This colonial policy and exploitation formed the cultural hallmark that renders the African women vulnerable today.

• *Traditional School of Thought.* The Nigerian tradition, according to Obasi, a researcher, "tops the list." It created the male superiority and female subordination theory known as 'Patriarchy'. Here, men theorize that they are 'born to rule'. This belief system fosters the wife and daughter inheritance scheme where anything in skirt is separated from royal sits, wills, family heritages, and other socio-cultural goodies. It created underaged marriage for girls as well as the harmful widowhood practices that subject a young widow to inhuman treatment in the name of ascertaining her innocence.

Today, men feel entitled to command, make decisions and relegate the women to the kitchen and the 'other room'. Where a woman tries to become something outside the four walls of these rooms or speaks with the guts of Obasa, Sirleaf, Ransome Kuti, Okonjo; she gets threatened and harassed to silence.

• *Poverty in Africa.* Most people here live below the poverty line. Economic and other related powers are what some humans exert over their fellow humans as tools for oppressions and subjuga-tions. Women are often given sex as a condition for accessing certain places. Those who reject such conditions would be shown the door.

The inability of women to meet basic necessities or to be financially independent exposes them to violent marriage, sexual harassments, etc. Most women in the rural areas survive narrowly on petty trade. Others who work in public establishments are either owed or paid pittances. Girls are asked to hawk or work as house help in places where they eventually get raped. Parents ask their daughters to persevere rich, wife-beating husbands because of the financial sustenance they get.

Also, where a woman is either beaten or raped, there is need to seek justice but lack of fund to take care of the litigation cost is a setback. Hence, her rights remain violated and abused.

• *Weak Judicial System.* A lot of innocent Africans have gone to the gallows due to a weak and perverted judicial system. Many

Judges and Justices compromise on the table of justice for financial gains. Criminals are walking the streets of Africa like kings because they have the ability to bribe their ways out. No wonder a renowned Nigerian poet, Niyi Osundare wrote a poem titled "My Lord, Tell Me Where to Keep Your Bribe". Most times, justice is not accessible to poor women in Africa as there is often high cost of litigation. Where it takes eternity for a court to decide cases that bother on abuses and violations of inalienable rights, the victim's rights cannot be said to be guaranteed.

• *Trepid Press.* Where the press is not free, it fails in its duty to protect human rights from being infringed upon. Some media outlets boycott reporting and publishing events where women are beaten to death, where girls are asked to hawk wares to be able to finance the boys' education, where a widow is treated like a criminal, where a girl is forced to get married or have sex, et al. Thanks to the social media. The mainstream media most times, seem to work on the dictates of certain powerful characters. They hardly stretch their searchlights towards the women facing molestations in rural areas.

THE IMPACT OF DOMESTIC VIOLENCE AGAINST WOMEN IN AFRIC
According to World health Organisation (WHO), in a 2005 study on women's health and domestic violence, millions of women in Africa are affected by violence. The then UN Secretary- General, Koffi Annan declared in 2006 report thus "Violence against women and girls is a problem of pandemic proportions". Domestic violence leaves a woman vulnerable, subjugated and exploited. Incessant beatings inflict injuries and turn many African women into being physically challenged. Mary Kimani, a blogger on Africa Renewal

reported that: "A police officer, in December 2018, beat his wife, Betty to paralysis and brain damage. Betty died five months later on her 28th birthday".

Too many violation cases stack up like yams in courts. In Zimbabwe, six out of ten murder cases tried in the Harare High Court in 1998 were related to domestic violence. Forced marriage exposes maidens to child birth complications and diseases. The raped are eternally traumatized. Domestic violence has sent a lot of women to untimely graves. The Rule of Law and Democracy are bastardized where human rights are not given their premium. Huge money is spent as legal fees. Violation of human rights undervalues the constitutions and laws of the land, even international laws in which these rights are enshrined.

COWING DOMESTIC VIOLENCE AGAINST WOMEN TO SUBMISSION

There have been many declarations, campaigns and activisms, but the problem seems to be multiplying. This 'problem of pandemic proportion' can be reduced to the barest minimum if not eradicated.

Women should be economically and culturally empowered not to be over reliant on men, even in their submissions as wives. The cultural norms should be reviewed to favour everyone regardless of gender.

Women and others should be well educated and informed about their rights in order to stand for them. In South Africa, Bill of Rights protects the rights of every South African. In Nigeria, Chapter 4 of the 1999 Constitution of the Federal Republic of Nigeria provides for the inalienable rights of citizens. The AU's Banjul Charter on human and people's rights. The UN Charters 1, 8, 13, 55, 62, 68 et al. provide for the human rights of all irrespective of race, religion and geography.

Also, in Nigeria, Section 19 of the Violence against persons Acts 2015 which prohibits spousal battery should be in action. The liability or punishment in 19(1) which includes 3-year imprisonment or a fine of N200,000 or both should not be escaped by the offenders.

The judiciary should be independent in its interpretations. The legal process should not be too expensive for redress. Law enforcement agents should be well approachable. The press should work without fear or favour towards ensuring that no human right goes violated.

CONCLUSION

Non-governmental organisations (NGOs) and other human/ women rights activists should not relent in their campaigns against the gross domestic violence daily militating against the wellbeing of African women. The African homes should be less violent. Boys should be trained to love and treat their sisters with respect. All mechanisms already in place to tame human rights violations and abuse should be effective implemented.

REFERENCES

- *Obasi, E (1997) "Structural Adjustment and Gender Access to Education in Nigeria"Gender and Education, 19 161-177.*
- *1999 Constitution of the Federal Republic of Nigeria hand book United Nations Charter (google).*
- *Sede Alonge, a writer on the Guardian (opinion), "Why are more African women more at risk of violence"?*
- *Mary Kimani (2007), "International norms, local activism start to alter laws, attitudes". African Renewal.*

• *Section 19 of the Violence Against Persons Act 2015-Ogunyemi, Adetunji (2015) "A Historical Reconstruction of the Colonial Government in Nigeria", 1940-1957. Retrieved Jan., 2nd, 2017.*

OSHO TUNDE *is a native of Ibadan, Oyo State, Nigeria. He is a writer and an undergraduate of Yaba College of Technology, where he studies Accounting. He is also an award-winning poet. His works have appeared on Praxis Magazine, Conscio, The Quills and elsewhere.*

GENDER-BASED VIOLENCE AND TRAFFICKING OF HUMAN PERSONS

OLUWATOBILOBA GRACE LAWALSON

Human rights are standards that recognize and protect the dignity of all human beings. The essence of existing not defined by gender, background, cultural inclination, sexuality or religion is guaranteed by human rights that should be always protected. They govern how we live in the society and with each other, as well as the relationship we have with the state and its obligation towards us. Contributing to the establishment of human rights system in Africa are the United Nations, international laws and the African Union which have positively influenced the betterment of the human rights situation in the African continent.

Human rights are enshrined in The Universal Declaration on Human Rights. These rights are broadly divided into the International Covenant on Civil and Political Rights and The International Covenant on Economic, Social and Cultural Rights. The Universal Declaration on Human Rights is the primary international legal source of civil, political, economic, social and cultural rights and these rights are an integral part of the documents that form the body of work which countries must have in local laws that are joint signatories of this agreement.

The Civil and Political Rights are rights to freedom of all forms of discrimination, equality before the law and equal protection of the law, life, prohibition of torture and cruel, inhuman and degrading treatment, personal liberty, fair trial and hearing, freedom of thought, religion and conscience; freedom of association and movement, freedom of association and speech, freedom to vote and be voted for and to acquire property or dispose at will.

The Economic, Social and Cultural Rights are rights concerning the basic social and economic conditions needed to live a life of dignity and freedom like pensions and old age care for the elderly as well as social security concerning unemployment, related to work, employment and workers' rights, health, sickness benefits and welfare of the disabled and the displaced; education, food, water, housing, and culture.

In Africa, we are governed regionally by the African Charter on Human and Peoples Rights, and there are established measures in the Charter that are supposed to safeguard people's right. The Charter has been ratified by 54 out of 55 African countries, meaning that these rights should be enforced in every state that has ratified it. Nigeria is part of this agreement and as a result, we have these laws in the constitution of the Federal Republic of Nigeria 1999 as amended. In the constitution of Nigeria, the civil and political rights are contained in Chapter 4 of the constitution while the economic, social and cultural rights are contained in Chapter 2 which deals with fundamental objectives and directive principles of state policy. They are listed as political, economic, social, educational, foreign policy and environmental objectives.

Unfortunately, while all these are the plethora of laws that many African countries have ratified, including Nigeria, who is also a party to the ratification of the Convention on the Elimination of all forms of Discrimination against Women, and the Optional Protocol Convention on the Elimination of all forms of Discrimination against Women ratified in 1985 and 2004 respectively, women still suffer gross human rights abuse in the country as they form the majority of people who suffer from trafficking and domestic violence in Africa and Nigeria. Some of this violence and trafficking are done by spouses, relatives, people in authority, law enforcement officers, parents and guardian, religious leaders etc. and actions are not brought due to fear and societal shame of the victims.

Many regulatory protocols that are supposed to make these procedures easy for women are fraught with loopholes that make it easy for abusers to walk away freely and the evidence gathering process relies mainly on all the efforts of the victim. These processes increase inhuman dignity, violate the right against torture, cruel and inhuman treatment contravening their fundamental human rights.

Domestic abuse can be sexual and physical like rape, molestation, assault, female genital mutilation and battery, in extreme cases choking, burns and disfigurement that can lead to death or verbal, emotional, psychological, mental or health challenges and trauma. Rape violates the liberty of person to select whether or not to have sexual relations with somebody, and anybody who violates such human rights should be subjected to serious punishments by the law. Some perpetrators are covered under matrimonial cloaking of the sanctity of marriage with laws not allowing women to sue their husbands despite statistics showing that women are abused by intimate partners or forced to marry perpetrators to avoid shame and stigma. Extreme cases of domestic abuse lead to ultimately paying with the most important price being the right to life.

According to the World Bank, gender-based violence is a global pandemic that affects at least 1 in 3 women. 35 percent of women worldwide have experienced either physical and/or sexual intimate partner violence or non-partner sexual violence. Globally, 7 percent of women have been sexually assaulted by someone other than a partner and as many as 38 percent of murders of women are committed by an intimate partner. 200 million women have experienced female genital mutilation/cutting.

Most African countries, after ratifying the economic, social and cultural rights, still look for means to ensure that they are not culpable for the full implementation of these laws increasing the incidence of gross violation of human rights. For example in Nigeria, with how lofty the fundamental objectives and directive principles of state policy which are our social, economic and cultural rights, the government cannot be forced to do them due to another section of the Nigerian Constitution. Section 6 where the powers of the judiciary are vested, specifically in subsections (6)(c), which states that:

- *The judicial powers vested in accordance with the foregoing provision of this section shall not, except as otherwise provided by this section, extend to any issues or questions as to whether any act or omission by any authority or person or as to whether any law or any judicial division is in conformity with the Fundamental objectives and directive principles of state policy set out in section II of this constitution.*

Trafficking violates the right to suitable employment, workers employment right as women are forced to trade their body in exchange for money and it tramples on their right to human dignity. Governments, in trying not to be held accountable for the economic, social and cultural rights in most African countries, who have such high levels of unemployment and underemployment, leave the most vulnerable who are not sent to school or cannot earn a living to be forced into trafficking where they are sexually abused and violated.

According to the Counter Trafficking Data Collaborative 2019 report, women and girls form about 80 percent of trafficking cases in the world with about 50 percent being under the age of 26. The most prevalent human right abuses faced include forced labour and sexual exploitation among other types of exploitation.

In Nigeria for example, section 17 which is for social objectives, specifically 17(3) states that The State shall direct its policy towards ensuring that all citizens, without discrimination on any group whatsoever, have the opportunity for securing adequate means of livelihood as well as adequate opportunity to secure suitable employment. Government allows for the perpetuation of the abuse of human rights by failing to provide employment or to cater for unemployment by providing social security for the unemployed. When there is no social security, people are forced to secure themselves through whatever ways that they seem fit, sometimes to the detriment of others and the society at large.

The responsibility is on us all to call on the government to be accountable to her citizens who need her to protect her. More stringent punishments need to be put in place for abusers with prosecution and punishment of offenders seen to be done, less procedural regulations that ridicule women making it hard for them to have access to justice, as well as ratifying laws in local states up to the grassroots to ensure protection at all levels, not minding religious or cultural leaning that usually seem to discriminate women and perpetuate abuse because of social and cultural preservation at the expense of the victim.

There is also the need to massively educate women by holding campaigns, educating through news and media outlets, at schools, in the educational curriculums, promptly investigate violations and influence policy if not laws that empower women so they can easily get help whenever necessary.

OLUWATOBILOBA GRACE LAWALSON *is a legal practitioner called to the Nigerian Bar, and a development professional. She is a Fellow of Platform Young Professional and is passionate about the development of Africa.*

HUMAN RIGHTS ABUSE AND VIOLATION IN AFRICA

OKAFOR MOSES ONYEBUCHI

Almost every African would consent to the fact that the phrase, 'human rights' is commonly used in many countries in Africa. Ranging from election manifestos to primary school education, the average African has always been reminded of the existence of certain fundamental rights, which have been granted to every African and protected by the government.

However, the frequent usage of the phrase is more than its application in Africa. Hence, a lot of Africans now regard such words as myths, rather than privileges they should enjoy, throughout their existence on earth.

The Oxford Learner's Dictionary defines Human Rights as one of the basic rights that everyone has, to be treated fairly and not in a cruel way, especially by their government. However, most dictionaries refer to the word 'right' as a 'privilege'. Nevertheless, when addressing the issue of human rights, we are talking about something that is more basic.

Every individual is entitled to basic fundamental rights, so long as they are human beings. These are called human rights rather than "human privileges" (which can be whisked away at someone's whim). They are called rights because they are things one is allowed to do, to have or to be. These rights are there to ensure protection against the attack of those who might want to harm or hurt human beings. Human rights are provisions that enable us get along with each other and live in harmony.

Several Africans know something about their rights. Generally, these persons believe that they have the right to food and a home. They also accept that they have a right to be paid wages for their labour. However, human rights are not limited to these things as there are many other rights.

When the people do not know their rights, they give room for all forms of abuses and violations such as discrimination, intolerance, injustice, oppression and slavery. No doubt, this has remained one of the major problems of the African majority, and a basic contributor to the violation of human rights in the continent.

The history of human rights abuse in Africa predates many generations. While in most civilisations, human rights abuse was very prominent and easily recognized; in some other civilisations, they were seen as the norm and people had no say on such issues. However, one of the earliest and most prominent incidents of human rights abuse in the continent was the racist system of apartheid in South Africa, which lasted for 46 years. The White-ruled South African Nationalist Party was one of the first modern abusers of human rights in Africa. The regime displayed a high resentment for equality in Africa, and classified the African man as a lesser being. Their treatment of South African from 1948 to 1994, remains one of the notable examples of human rights violation.

However, the rise of political advocate and revolutionary, Nelson Mandela, became the saving grace of the nation. His fight for equality in his country is very much admirable today, and a great inspiration to many Africans. South Africans are free today and enjoy their basic rights, due to the input of this great icon and legend—a proof that human rights abuse can be curbed anywhere it is found.

After the apartheid era, White-Black oppression was somehow done on a limited scale, with major incidences of human rights abuse in Africa occurring among Africans. The new age saw the rise of many hard-hearted politicians, and heads of states who turned democracy to oppression. The likes of Saddam Hussein, Idi Amin of Uganda and General Sani Abacha are all in the bad books of Africans. Nevertheless, even bad things come to an end, as these politicians also left their evil legacy for the call beyond. Unfortunately, their deaths have not stopped the occurrence of human rights in the continent.

The innate nature of domination that has remained a major component of man is still being displayed in many fronts.

Nowadays, human rights abuse and violation has been renamed as shooting of peaceful protesters, child soldiers, rigging election results among many others in Africa. The surprising fact is that Africans have become weary from the continual suppression of their rights, and have resorted to accepting evil as good. Little wonder, they are quick to compare the continent with other developed continents, where human beings are valued and human rights expressed. The use of peaceful protests by the people to voice their opinions in other continents is scarcely obtainable in Africa. Events such as the End SARS Protest and the Sudan Protests show that once power is given to one in Africa, power is taken from all.

Certainly, no better examples illustrate the exhibition of human rights abuse and violation than the nations of Africa. In most parts of the continent, certain events such as forced marriage, genital mutilation and forced religion still occur, despite the massive development the world is experiencing. Some countries are even vocal about their resentment for the female gender, and their restriction of the basic rights of human.

It is pathetic to see that a woman is denied access to certain things, simply because she is a woman and not a man. The popular African adage, "What a man can do, a woman can do better" has become a mere rhythm in the continent, because there is no room for its application. Hence, violent abuses of human rights such as rape, groping and sexual molestation are more directed towards the females, due to the existence of gender inequality in the continent. The male gender is not entirely excluded from this menace. Issues, such as delay in payments of salary, random shootings, and killings by unknown gunmen or uniformed men and Fulani Herdsmen oppressions still affect the male gender.

Surprisingly, most of these attacks even come from sources expected to protect the masses. There have been widespread cases of soldiers or police officers molesting civilians, without considering the consequences of their actions; due to the fact that the uniform is now more powerful than the judge.

The major issue of concern is that the government is reluctant in addressing these issues, and in most cases, the elected leaders are the main causes of the problem; which has made it impossible for them to solve these problems. Notwithstanding, a proper approach to human rights abuse in Africa will surely produce an admirable result for the continent. Obviously, the solution to this problem is readily available, but applying them is the difficult part for many Africans.

One of such solutions is the enlightenment of every African on their rights and the implementation of these rights. Africa has been known to focus more on education of human rights than application. Hence, people know their rights, but cannot exercise their rights.

Therefore, implementation should start from even the least among us. The young child in the primary school should be allowed to enjoy his or her basic rights, and should not be denied of any of these human rights.

More so, the masses should embrace tactical approaches to subverting wrong government policies, and the use of protests should be minimized. Bad governance thrives very much in an atmosphere of fear; hence, removing such individuals would require the aid of higher authorities that these government officials would be afraid of challenging.

Finally, Africans must embrace unity, integrity and resilience in the fight for the restoration of our basic human rights. Corruption among the masses must be terminated, in order to bring down the corrupt government officials, who promote the abuse of these basic human rights. No doubt, if Africans could emulate the lives of most successful revolutionaries and embrace change, human rights abuse and violation would become history in the continent. For as they say, 'United we stand, and divided we fall. We can fight it; we just need to stand up for our rights.

OKAFOR MOSES ONYEBUCHI *is a student of University of Nigeria, Nsukka. He is passionate about writing and currently works as a content creator, in combination with his studies.*

HUMAN RIGHTS ABUSE AND VIOLATION IN AFRICA

ODHIAMBO JERAMEEL KEVINS OWUOR

According to an array of scholars, human rights are rights inherent to all humans irrespective of their race, social status, and nationality, area of origin, tribe, language, colour or intellectual origin. By virtue that one is a human, he or she is entitled to enjoy these rights and no one should infringe or deny them any rights whatsoever. No one is to be discriminated on the basis of the aforementioned ills. Further, these rights are indivisible, interrelated and interdependent on each other. This means that there should be at no any point selective application of the various rights one is entitled to enjoy. Whether one is poor or rich, he or she must be guaranteed his or her rights. This is the duty of the state in question and whenever they do deny the public of their rights without justifiable reason there must be legal implication on the said government.

One may ask what the source of the human rights is. Human rights overtime have been developed from international laws and then domesticated by various countries by virtue of them being member states of the various international bodies. As well, these rights to some extent are expressed in treaties, customary international law and international human rights laws. Each member state of the international bodies that have ratified and passed various legislations on human rights is entitled to protect human rights and fundamental freedoms of their individual citizens. One of the greatest tenets of human rights is that it is universal and inalienable. Many intellectuals do posit that the principle of universality is the cornerstone of international human rights law.

The bedrock of the international human rights framework consists of three documents namely; Universal Declaration of Human Rights, The International Convention on Civil and Political Rights and The International Covenant on Economic, Social and Cultural Rights. In Africa the major source of Human Rights is African Charter on Human and Peoples Rights which is also known as Banjul Charter. Despite coming up of several international instruments so as to mitigate the abuse of human rights; it is apparent that there has been a wide spread violation of human rights. This means that several governments in Africa, to be specific, are sitting on their laurels and are adamant to ensure that there is full compliance with the international instruments as well as the Constitutions which contain Bill of Rights.

The major causes of human rights abuse in Africa do include; police brutality, political instability, economic scarcity, prohibition of same sex activities, domestic violence, racial discrimination, state capture of the Judiciary, denial of various freedoms, illegal evictions and lack of freedom of the press.

During each and every cycle of elections in African states, it is always a sure bet that the ruling government will make sure that the opposition will never thrive. They do this by arresting opposition politicians, torturing the opposition, denying them freedom of movement by putting them under house arrest, initiating dubious suits in court so as to silence the opposition and even at times killing the opposition. This leads to anarchy, thus leading to civil wars. A key example of the same in the recent past has been in Uganda, Tanzania and Kenya. Last year, Ghana did show the way, for the sitting President His Excellency Nana Akufo Addo did not in way maim his opposition, led by former President John Mahama.

Domestic violence in Africa has been on the rise courtesy of the patriarchal nature of our individual cultures. This has led to some women being killed, injured and some are suffering in their various homes. The civil societies have tried so as to mitigate this despite the rise of the same.

Female Genital Mutilation has led to ladies losing their dignity. This is forced on them for they hail from communities which do practice the art so they cannot say no. Yet it causes pain to the ladies, leads to complication of their sexual and reproductive organs and it has led to death of several persons. Many of those who are arrested for practicing the same are not as well punished for the same.

Police Instability has been the new cancer it has led to many joining ancestors in the land of no return yet they still have more time on the surface of the earth. Right to life is one of the rights that are given priority, for without it one cannot enjoy other rights at all. The police do defy this and at times use live bullets on protestors who have a valid reason and licence for industrial action. Judiciary ideally is supposed to be the custodian of laws and various rights. They are envisioned to do this by safeguarding the laws. That is not the situation in Africa. The independence of the Judiciary is only in the books and it is never in practice. This has led to the government evicting masses out of their own land and other atrocities. They do this with the full knowledge that nothing will be done to them.

Ethics and Professional code of journalism or press dictates that they should be reporting the correct information as it is on the ground whether it is good or bad. The governments of various African countries have made sure that the press never state what is negative to the government at all cost. Those who publish or report what the government feels like will make masses to be aggrieved against them; they (the government) would make sure that they (the press) are arrested, terminated and taken to court. The freedom of the press is on its deathbed in various African countries.

Courtesy of the firm African beliefs and traditions added to the religion that most Africans believe in; most African states have been reluctant to make provisions for same sex activities. In the introduction of this essay, I did highlight candidly that all are to enjoy human rights and no one should be discriminated on the basis of the same at all cost. When one decides to belong to LQBT+, he or she should be left to enjoy her union. Unfortunately this is not the case in Africa; in fact in Uganda belonging to that group is a death sentence.

In a nutshell despite the numerous legislations, international instruments and constitutions, the story of human rights violations seems to never change. It is evident that there is lack of political goodwill in most instances and those who are in the apex leadership positions. That means that the laws are perfect but the biggest problems comes with implementation of the same.

To mitigate this, there is need to encourage adherence to the law (no situational ethics), the various states should guarantee economic, social and political rights to all and sundry within their jurisdiction. Moreover human equality, dignity and peace should be at top of priority to ensure a better coexistence of masses. There is need for human rights to be upheld at all cost, for that is the dictate of the law and those who infringe or deny people their rights should be subjected to strict punishment.

We still stand a chance to rewrite the story, the past maybe be filthy but at least we have a future on a clean slate where we can aim to achieve human rights for all.

ODHIAMBO JERAMEEL KEVINS OWUOR *is a Law student at the University of Nairobi School of Law, Parklands Campus, Kenya.*

ISSUE WITH THE FREEDOM OF EXPRESSION BY ACTIVISTS

ODE CONFIDENCE

When there is dearth of fatherhood in a family, the family must most times lives without tongue. The effect of human right abuse on the activists within Nigeria and Africa context as well as the world has left the society in a desert of more abuse.

The larger human society occupied by the poor masses is like the family in my analogy above, that lives without a father. In essence, the certainty that those who have stood up (or attempted to stand up against human rights abuse) have affected not only human right of those individuals, but also proffers the larger society the loaming future that will be a rather bizarre threat to human right.

Human rights are rights enshrined in the constitution of a state to guide its citizenry from unlawful torture and punishment. They are fundamental to all persons, as Merriam Webster dictionary puts. These rights are constitutional as regards to the freedom of the people living in a particular society.

According to Merriam-Webster Dictionary, human right abuse is the violation of those basic rights of people by treating them wrongly. To violate or abuse human rights is to carry out practices which are outside the law. The act of violation of the rights of humans is no longer considered humane and thus violators are not to be found in any human society. Examples of the basic human rights include: the right to life, right to freedom of association, and most importantly, the right to freedom of expression, which is topical here.

My focus here is to draw our attention to the violation of human rights of the activists, who have seen the mysterious excruciation of the masses and have decided to lend their voices to protect their rights from abuse. It is pertinent to note that such act of abuse on human affects Africa negatively. The activists, as metaphorically represented in the above analogy as fathers, play major role in the protection of the right of their people through political, economic and socio-cultural critiquing. They are the answers to the cry of the praying poor masses who desire better treatment rather than torture, long suffering, starvation, forceful eviction of their children, child abuse, inequality and the deprivation of the dividend of the natural resources at their disposal.

Activists are intellectuals, who are often inclined towards righting wrongs, and as a result they tend to speak against inhumane approaches in the society. These individuals are members of our society, who are conscious of the socio-reality of the people. Thus, they rise to agitate for good governance, equality in the distribution of resources in most cases (using Nigeria as a case in view). And, above all, they protect the rights of the people, in order to maintain justice and fairness. Most importantly they call for a society free from political marginalization.

There are notable personalities who are considered activists because of their benevolence and quest for a better society. Some of such individuals in Nigeria and Africa at large include Nelson Mandela, Desmond Tutu, Dele Giwa, Thomas Sankara, Wole Soyinka, Ken Benule Beeson Saro Wiwa, Kiki Mordy, Gani Fawehinmi, Omoyele Sowore, to mention but a few. These persons lend out their voices and carry out revolutionary movements geared towards blotting out non-human treatments by anti-human government officials, and human rights violators in Nigeria and other African countries. These voices are the earnest prayers of the populace who desire equality (in resource distribution, as in the case of the Niger Delta) and also the protection of their rights. Activists carry out movements in order to scrutinize violators of human rights and lift up the burden of the masses.In Africa, activists are denied the freedom of expression which is considered human rights abuse. History has it that Nelson Mandela who was a democratic and anti apartheid leader was imprisoned for twenty seven years because of exercising his right to fight against bad governance, and protect the right of his people from political marginalisation. This act of abuse and violation is common in the African society. There are considerable number of instances of torture, detention, treason, arrest, false allegations and prosecution of activists in the Nigeria and Africa at large. The issue with such non humanistic practice is that it will hamper the development of Africa as a continent, leave the people (poor masses) with political or socio-cultural apathy and no sense of belonging; increase the rate/number of suicide, and cause untold suffering and war even with the availability of resources in Africa, Unionism; and true democracy will be far from our continent.

Nigeria as the giant of Africa as well as a country with vast geographical land, abundant natural resources, example, oil and gas, and the most populated Black nation, just like other countries in Africa has record of the instances of abuse of rights against human, political, social and environmental right activists. As was documented by the Human Right Watch, an example is the arrest, beating and detention of Omoyele Sowore.

Omoyele Sowore, a Nigerian human right activist and the founder of an online news platform known as Sahara Reporters, is a victim of human right abuse and violation by the anti-human or violators of human rights as a result of carrying out a protest, which is not a crime, as enshrined in the Constitution Article 19 of the Human Right Law. Sowore, who spoke on the 29th of September 2020 during a news briefing, expressed his grievance on how he was tortured and locked in a dark room for five months, where he was restricted and denied all his rights, simply because he planned to carry out a nationwide protest against bad governance.

As is known, protest in every society is geared towards bringing about social, economic, political change as well as to put an end to bad governance, corruptible practices, inequality and to promote peaceful co-existence which is a lacking factor in the political and social structure of Nigeria. But often times, the military agencies display acts which are non humanistic to protesters and their leaders (activists) by arresting, shooting directly at protesters, delay trial and even killing of the activists. This is indeed the abuse of human rights because it is clearly enshrined in the Nigerian Constitution in section 39(1) that citizens are entitled to freely express themselves.

Omoyele Sowore had been severally arrested by the Nigerian State Security Service. On one occasion, he was arrested on the 3rd of August 2019, and accused of treason. Again on the 1st of January 2020, he was arrested, beaten and badly tortured because he intended to carry out a protest tagged #RevolutionNow.

"Who has benefited? There is no basic healthcare; we don't have running water; we don't have electricity. Right now, Nigeria is a leaking basket," Sowore once said.

This had been his revolutionary expression which brought him torture and brutality by the armed forces, which is considered as violation of human right.

Away from Omoyele Sowere, other activists have risen at different times, and have in one way or the other become victims of the menace of human right abuse, one of whom is Kenule Beeson Ken Saro Wiwa, an environmental activist of the Niger Delta area of Nigeria. Ken Saro Wiwa, lent his voice to his people (Ogoni) against exploitation and environmental degradation. He was killed by hanging after being accused of murder. History has it that after his death, the people confessed that they where bribed to accused him of being a murderer. Ken Saro Wiwa, the President of the Movement for the Survival of the Ogoni People (MOSOP) was executed during the Sani Abacha Military Regime on the 15th of November 1995.

In 1967, Wole Soyinka a political activist was imprisoned by his act of resilience by the Nigerian Military government for a period of 22 months.

Dele Giwa was killed by a mail bomb in his residence in October 19th 1986. There are still other numerous instances of death of activists which have instilled fear in intellectuals who would have stood to tell the truth. Africa will remain a dark continent if there are regular torture, detention, delay trial and prosecution of those who serve the purpose of fatherhood. Therefore, all anti-human agencies should shun abuse and denial of the activists' right of freedom of expression which is a mechanism to the exposure of bad governance.

Conclusively, the theme of Human Right Abuse cannot be exhausted especially when there is restriction to the number of words in an essay like this. It is time when all African would come together and put a stop to human right abuse and its perpetrators. There are different forms of abuses like that of police brutality, and killing of the #EndSARS protesters which left us (Nigerians) with an unforgettable day in history, (the Lekki Toll Gate Massacre of 20th October, 2020). However, the issue with the lack of freedom of expression by activist as a form of human right abuse is a salient one and should be snithed out of our society, in order to build an abuse-free Africa of our dream.

ODE CONFIDENCE *is an English and Communication Arts student of Ignatius Ajuru University of Education. He is an essayist, poet and a trainee teacher with the vision to cause a desirable change in his country and Africa. He is also a member of Society of Young Nigerian Writers, IAUE Branch.*

HUMAN RIGHTS ABUSE AND VIOLATIONS IN AFRICA

OBEBE OLUSOJI

The protection of human rights in most African countries is never a guaranteed exercise. Beyond reasonable doubt, encroachment on human rights has been the order of the day. But the historical fact is that Africans have long been deprived of their rights in the hands of the white. It is not untrue that the white colonial masters degraded the humanness of the Africans. Humanness, here, is a prerequisite to enjoying natural rights and liberties. Each African's personalness and worth have been dragged through the mire as a result of slavery and inhuman treatment which negate the articles 4, 5 and 7 of the UDHR (Universal Declaration of Human Right, 1948). This, therefore, introduces the contemporariness of the right abuse trend in Africa.

The era of this historical backdrop closes as soon as the Africans break free from the shackles of colonialism which have held them bound from exercising their rights. The year 1960, in the words of Dag Hammarskjold (former Secretary General of UN), is the "Year of Africa". In this remarkable year, about seventeen African countries have become independent.

Nevertheless, with the emancipation in place, the dent is still left uncleared. Over the years, the experience of independence even worsens the abuse and violation of human rights. The past and present governments that appear in African countries, especially in the year 1960s, 1970s and 1980s, have been a set of leaders militating against peoples' enjoyment of their rights. They put the people under the duress of fear as if exercising or fighting for human rights is a felony.

In Ghana, the Nkrumah-led Administration, in 1958, enacted the Prevention Detention Act which allowed the government to arrest and detain any person without trial. Likewise in the present-day Nigeria, the current government poses a great threat to human rights. When the president, Muhammadu Buhari, emerged as the Military Head of State in 1983 to 1985, many great Nigerians, such as Tunde Thompson and Nduka Irabor of the Guardian Newspaper fell victim of his resistance towards human rights exercise.

Although, most military governments have no or little respect for citizens' rights, the above recapitulation is necessary to substantiate that the civilian government of Nigeria now under the said President is just a reflection of his military leadership as shown recently in the case of the Nigerian human right activist, Owoyele Sowore and a few others coupled with the gruesome pressure mounted on the youths for coming out to fight for their rights against police brutality. Even when the system of government practised is Democracy—a system in which the rights of the people are entrenched in the constitution—the African governments still take absolute control and decisions on determining the way these rights are to be exercised. This effects a strict limit set to the exhibiting of human rights, if not an utmost denial.

Meanwhile, the judiciary which is assumed to be the last hope of the common man, and the courts that are presented as the protectors of human rights have lost their independence in Africa. The courts of law are to see to the dispensation of justice but the reverse is the case with African countries. Just like the rhetorical question asked by Saint Augustine in his "City of God" (353 –430 AD): "Without justice, what is a state but a robber band". The judiciary in all African states virtually is nothing but a mere rubber-stamped body of legal figureheads. It is either a matter of executive government control or bribery and corruption.

Cases of unfair hearings and unjust court proceedings are prevalent in Africa. There is no doubt that the main purpose of the judiciary has been thwarted. As Kayode Eso JSC emphasised, "There is no justification for the existence of the judiciary except in its existence for the defence of the citizen, for the citizen to put his view across with all potency... for him to feel and breathe the air of freedom around him." The judicial systems of African countries, however, have lost independence as they now deny people's right to fair hearing and justice. This is displayed in the case of Abdelwahab Fersaoui, President of the Youth Action Rally (Algeria) arrested and charged with 'compromising the integrity of the national territory', while his lawyer keeps writing for his release; but yet, his trial has not been scheduled.

Moreover, in Africa, poverty is very common and still lingering. An estimate shows that there are about 433 million poor people in Africa. Another one from Bloomberg reveals that Africa may have 90% of the world's poor by 2030. And poverty is one way of having one's rights deprived or denied. While in London's Trafalgar Square in 2005, Nelson Mandela said that to overcome poverty is an act of justice; the protection of human right, the right to dignity and a decent life. He also added that "While poverty persists, there is no true freedom". These statements are true and valid in regards to Africa's situation. It is only in Africa that people buy justice at the detriment of those who should have it. In the real sense, poor people cannot boast of their rights or have them safeguarded. In fact, the poor are just subjects; the rich are really the citizens. A poor African man who is fighting for his rights is only trying to attract more misfortunes because his voice will never be heard. The poor are the voiceless, usually shut up by the oppressiveness of the rich.

In furtherance to this end, what has befallen many Africans that lack political education is the denial of their rights. Some will not have anything to do with court matters. Many will shudder at the hearing of 'Police'. They don't know all these agencies are established for the realisation of human rights. Hence, because of their ignorance, they become the vulnerable set.

Although other countries in the world such as America, Australia, UK, France, China, etc. are faced with the problem of human rights abuse and violations, that of the African continent has been so persistent and bestial. The aforementioned cases are all an attestation to this fact.

OBEBE OLUSOJI *is a Nigerian poet and writer. At present, he works as an auxiliary teacher. His writings are mostly penned for the promotion of humanity.*

A MORTAL CARNAGE

NWOKEABIA, IFEANYI JOHN

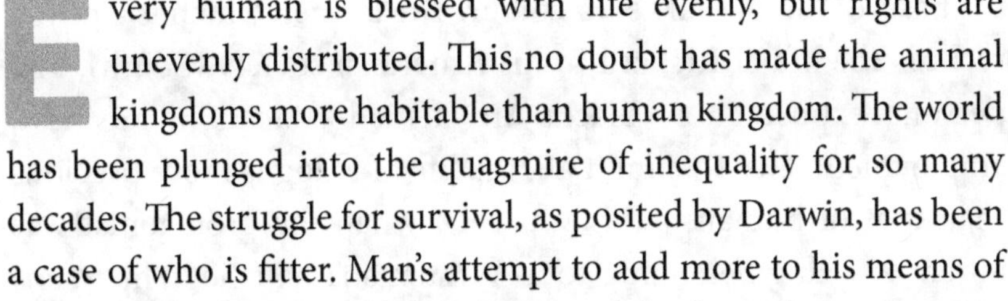

Every human is blessed with life evenly, but rights are unevenly distributed. This no doubt has made the animal kingdoms more habitable than human kingdom. The world has been plunged into the quagmire of inequality for so many decades. The struggle for survival, as posited by Darwin, has been a case of who is fitter. Man's attempt to add more to his means of livelihood brought out the discovery of the later days countries, which were subjected to be ruled by stronger countries. 'A child who defeated another rarely allows it breath of life'; so those subject countries were treated badly by the colonising countries.

Anywhere a person is born, he has become a citizen of that place. Then, a person's parents' country of origin determines the origin of the person. Originality of individuals has constituted great problem in the abuse of rights of such individuals. Human rights abuse, according to Merriam's Webster dictionary, is violation of the basic rights of people by treating them wrongly.

As a citizen of a particular country, you are entitled to some certain privileges, but once those things are denied of you, then you are purely less a human. If we are to take a look at Biblical account of creation, there's never a place that it's stipulated that God created 'White' or 'Black'; rather we are told that He created a man (human).

Furthermore, the Bible always attributes humans with their country of origin like; 'Samaritan Woman', 'Ethiopian Eunuch', etc. Where did humans learn 'White' or 'Black'? These two colours have caused humans unbearable torture over a long period of time.'

'Black Boy' by Richard Wright and 'Sizwe Bansi is Dead' by Athol Fugard et al are two powerful books amongst many, written to expose the evil human rights abuse and violation just on the basis of individual's skin colour. The former, which is a novel, records the life of Richard in his American society (South). The persona exposes how Blacks are denied education, business, employment, etc. To sum it all, the life of a dog is more precious than that of humans—this was seen when the protagonist was bitten by a dog belonging to a 'Whiteman'; he (the Whiteman) laughed it over that a dog bite can do anything to a Black. So, last year 2020, a black American, George Floyd, was murdered by a police who ought to protect him. It sparked off protest in America, with many taking to the streets to speak against the canker. According to CNN, April 2014 witnessed a racist abuse on Dani Alves who was then Barcelona player on their crucial match against Villarreal. He was stoned a banana (monkey shares so much relationship with banana). In a tweet by a teammate, Neymar, after the match, "Dani Alves owned him," tweeted the Brazilian's teammate Neymar. "Take that bunch of Racists. We are all Monkeys So What?"

On other hand, Athol Fugard's 'Sizwe Bansi is Dead' exposes the abuse and violation of rights and privileges of the 'Blacks' by the 'Whites'. Apartheid reigned so supreme in South Africa that a man was denied right to travel to some parts of his country except if he had obtained permit to. Those who served diligently their country are retired with a gold wristwatch. They are denied opportunities to participate in the decision making of their country. This is a case of one becoming a stranger in his or her land of origin, thereby soliciting direction from strangers.

The opening sentence of Rousseau in 'The Social Contract', "Man is born free, and everywhere he is in chains" comes handy in this discussion. They would always tell you that you are free, but when you check well, you will discover that prison is such a beautiful place to be in. Africa has become in the recent times 'a den of human abusers'. This may be looked at as an overgeneralization, but a keen look will open our eyes to the horrifying news trailing our daily radios, televisions and social media.

Nigeria in recent times is battling with an unending case of banditry. Banditry is a type of organised crime committed by outlaws typically involving the threat or use of violence. A person who engages in banditry is known as a bandit and primarily commits crimes such as extortion, robbery, and murder, either as an individual or in groups (Wikipedia). In some parts of Northern Nigeria, motorists no longer ply some roads because of the fear of bandits. Citizens are denied the freedom of movement because of some wicked individuals who wouldn't live to see others live in peace.

An Islamic sect led by Shekarau called Boko Haram is also seriously terrorising the entire country. They specialize in bombing and killing of innocent citizens who are either in churches or mosques worshipping God. They visit schools (like the case of Chibok) to abduct school children, thereby trampling on their human rights to life and education. Citizens live in fear. Everyone deserves to live a protected life, but in this case, life is no longer golden.

The citizens, last year, 2020, took to the streets to protest on the act of a certain police unit (SARS) for always infringing on the rights of people they are supposed to protect. When an individual is pushed to the wall, he can only but retaliate. The police's popular statement, "Police is your friend", became a serious protest and ironical mimicry, as many joked with it. People agitated for disbanding of SARS unit of police because of how they killed citizens without allowing them fair hearing in a reputable court of law. When a body saddled with the responsibility of protecting you turn out to be your killer; where will you run to for salvation?

Life cannot be perfectly defined, but we always rely on different societal definitions to model our lives. Who actually told people that homosexuals and lesbians are satanic? It's a case of one deriving joy in bitterleaf soup, while another seeking to enjoy the delightful taste of Okra soup. So, will you now say that one should be killed for his or her choice? Abusing or violating the rights of humans on the basis of their chosen sexual life shouldn't be allowed to hold water. Everyone is bound to live by the choice he or she has made. More so, the bisexual humans are mostly seen as unfit to be members of the society. The social stigma these individuals go through on daily basis is dehumanizing, and some of them end up committing suicide. This is how humans end up in killing other humans through their actions.

In conclusion, humans are meant to live life as free as they can, because God created life to be enjoyed freely. There's no hindrance to the air we breathe; the rich, the Black, the White and the poor enjoy the same piece of air without any discrimination. How can humans created by God now decide to go against another? Let's do away with abuse and all forms of violation of human rights so that we can enjoy a new freer world.

NWOKEABIA, IFEANYI JOHN *is a poet and teacher. He writes from Anambra State. He has Nigeria Certificate in Education and Bachelor of Arts in Education, both in English Language. His works are published in different online platforms.*

HUMAN RIGHTS IN AFRICA: THE LACUNA

JIDE OGUNLANA

Human rights are basic entitlements of the citizens and not privileges. One of the greatest contributions by the international community in ensuring social justice and peace in society is the Universal Declaration of Human Rights. It goes a long way in curbing the excesses of especially the leaders and in ensuring peaceful and orderly coexistence among people. But I believe that as ideal and laudable this Declaration is, as with many issues planted in different environments with peculiarities of cultures and traditions, the enforcement of these rights in individual countries globally is more easily encouraged than achieved. There are many factors that are considered a stranglehold on this Declaration in Africa and which must be attended to. I will highlight three of these factors in this essay, viz: poverty, illiteracy and African traditional values.

Until the fundamental issue of poverty is addressed, violation of human rights in Africa will not only continue to increase, but sadly, it will also be tolerated and it is the laws against it that will ironically be viewed as oppressive and offensive. When a governor in one of the states in the south-west of Nigeria was alleged to be dragging his feet in removing the hawkers from the streets, he revealed that he also hawked when he was a child to make ends meet. The tendency is that perhaps if the governor had not hawked for the poverty-stricken parents, he would not have been educated and his name would not have been heard beyond his village where he would be drinking palm wine after feeding his goats and chickens before they are safely locked in their coops for the night. Some parents may have to supplement the little they make with the profits their twelve-year-old child makes from hawking after the school hours before they can make ends meet. The Human Rights Declaration would call this child abuse but society would call it family survival. A good number of people would be ready to trade their right to vote for food they badly need in order to live. Freedom of association is greatly threatened through blackmailing when the will to practise the religion of one's choice is subverted when one has to embrace the religion of the employer to get a job badly needed. Most laws in many African countries allow for the right of a child to be educated but make no provision to cater for poverty-stricken parents or for free or totally free basic education for the children.

With regards to illiteracy, there is no gainsaying the fact that this is really an issue in Africa. According to African Union data, as of 2019, literacy rates in African countries are estimated to be 70%. Illiteracy is a real challenge to human rights. When an illiterate boy who neither knows his right as a human nor the wrong acts as a policeman is arrested by an African policeman, he is asked to pay some amount for his bail. The mother, who cannot live with the shame of her only son going to jail, is only too ready to pay the illegal money to get his son out after a week of illegal detention in police custody. Also, illiteracy makes it difficult for many people in Africa to get more profitable jobs. The easiest jobs to get in most African countries are labouring jobs where no qualification or experience is required. This however is accompanied with much human right violation by the employers. Impunity is rampant among many employers of labour and the security personnel. There are issues of unfair labour practices of the employers of labour in total disregard to the labour acts. This writer recognizes the immense contributions of foreigners in creating jobs for Africans in many African countries. In most instances, this however does not go without a great price to pay. Many of the established factories hire underage workers and it is not uncommon to witness issues of racial discrimination in the factories. The working conditions are in most cases unhealthy and inhuman and the pay grossly inadequate and unlawful, most of the time below the country's minimum wage. It must however be emphasized that these violations of human rights are not limited to only foreign employers of labour as many African-owned private companies and factories are equally guilty of these illegal and immoral acts. Since to the victim the job was heaven-sent as he could not get a better job which would demand paper qualifications and experience, he would prefer to cope with the hardship than bringing the human rights violation of his employers to the attention of the government for the fear of losing his job. Until the issue of illiteracy is addressed frontally with political will by the various governments in Africa, the sad reality is that violation of human rights would continue at work places for a long time to come.

Lastly, where do we draw the line between human rights and African traditional values? African traditional values of respect, as a point of reference, most of the time, conflict with the right to speech. In Africa, you are most of the time never seen as a grown up by your father or mother. In most communities such as that of the Yoruba people, you don't look into your parents' face when you talk to them. You don't talk when they are still talking; you keep quiet or you are considered recalcitrant. When a father in anger says, I am your father! what he is saying in essence is that he should know more than you do, as he has seen more and experienced more in life. But I have to be quick to say here that an average traditional African person will not envy the kind of freedom that most parents in western countries allow the children to enjoy. Bernard Shaw says one thing he likes about America is the way parents obey their children. A child inviting the police to come and arrest his own father, even for child abuse, though is not unheard of, is an aberration in African society. Such a child would be considered a bastard. While the point here is mainly to highlight the conflicts between human rights and the African value system and it is not within the scope of this essay to justify any communal practice, many would argue that the culture of respect even when it denies the child some rights, goes a long way in the preservation of traditional values, which makes for relatively more orderly and peaceful family relationship.

In conclusion, I am convinced there is a great resemblance in the idea of democracy as is, and should be, practised in the developed world and in Africa and The Universal Declaration of Human Rights. The Declaration recognizes the facts that although people differ in sex, race, colour of the skin and religion, everyone is entitled to enjoy certain human rights for the establishment of freedom, justice and peace all over the world. But then, the Declaration, just like the democracy idea, should also perhaps take into consideration various cultural, social and economic differences among these various nations of the world and find a way of addressing the lacuna to guarantee its complete success, the step, which if neglected, may not only make the ideas difficult to practise but also offensive in some African cultures. In a purely traditional African setting, it may be a choice, for instance, between communal peace and freedom of speech. Consequently, the freedom of speech may lose out. It may be a choice between the alarming divorce rate in the west and the husband calling the shots which makes for peace in a till-death-do-us part African marriage. There must be a way of reconciling all these. Also, at least in Nigeria, you would scarcely see anyone who is about 40 years old and above who would not have had to contribute to the family purse by hawking one thing or the other for the parents from as early as age 12. Most parents tell the young ones of nowadays this story of their childhood years to encourage hardwork in them, but this is labelled child abuse in the Declaration. While the writer recognizes the inherent danger of such practice, perhaps there should be a way to get round it, at least until the various African governments wake up to their responsibilities in addressing the evil of poverty in the continent. Getting more serious in providing free and quality education for these teeming children will also, to a long extent, bridge these gaps in the implementation of this Declaration in Africa.

Two of JIDE OGUNLANA'S *plays, Verbal Violence, and Clash of the Gods, have been successfully staged in the Arts Theatre of the University of Ibadan, Nigeria; and they are being read in some higher institutions in the country. He co-wrote Communicative English Studies for Senior Secondary Schools1-3, (2012). His storybook, Primrose and the Kidnappers, won the 2018 ANA Prize for Children's Literature. He has worked with Evans Brothers (Nig. Publishers) Ltd for some years before he founded his own publishing company where he now works as a writer, a rewriter and an editor. As a professional editor, he has edited works of some popular Nigerian writers, such as the prose works of Dr. Wale Okediran, the Secretary General of Pan African Writers Association (PAWA) and a former Member of Parliament; the biography of a former Governor of Oyo State; the fantasy novel of Diipo Fagunwa (the son of the D.O. Fagunwa), and the autobiography of Prof. Samuel Olusegun Ayodele, a renowned Nigerian professor of English.*

THE LOCUST IN AFRICA

INNOCENT CHIEMEZIE OHAEKWE

⸺⦿⸺

The ever existence and marauding nature of the fearless locust has since given rise to a society void of sanity and serene environment. A once lawful society now turned ironical. The locust in Africa is that giant walking statue, walking boldly on day broad light and infiltrating into the ethical codes of the society, thereby causing havoc and societal unrest.

Admittedly, no human society exists without challenges, obstacles and hindrances. Just like man and his problems, the society grows with its challenges, one of which is the marginalization, dehumanization and deprivation of Human Rights. Human Rights abuse has consistently been a major part of our existence contributing to the high rate of degradation in our society.

To my best understanding, an abuse or violation of the human right occurs when certain constitutional and natural rights of a person are deprived or denied from him/her. This results from many societal vices like racial discrimination, sexual abuse, political disorder, religious bigotry, cultural diversity, and most importantly the socio-political corruption that has eaten deep into the tenets and rubrics of African society.

Among Africans, corruption has become the most outstanding locust marauding through the African society and waging a war against the ordinary man as well as the progress of the society.

Emphatically, the ordinary man who represents the peasant's population in our African society happens to be the victim and core bearer of the cross which corruption has brought about. He is denied access to work in a much more exquisite office or position because he lacks what is known in the society as connection which is the only panacea that can accord him such prestigious positions. The ordinary man is deprived of his essential rights like the freedom of fair hearing and good livelihood. He is threatened and persecuted should he raise a voice in defence of his human right. Although, corruption has continued to run rampant in all corners of the African society, the rate at which our political overlords treat our individual rights is wholly injurious to our personalities. The bitter and ironical part of it is the wrongful use of our security agents who constitutionally should protect the lives and properties of the entire citizens but now turn against the lives they ought to defend. Recently in the Nigerian society, there was the youth uprising, popularly tagged #EndSARSProtest, where the marginalized youths stood out to protest against the evils of our political leaders and the excessive police brutalities. This exercise, no doubt, is their right, but they were silenced, killed and forced to withdraw by the same police agents sent by orders from above. This, I believe, is the highest level of infringement of human rights, which has since created a wound at the fingertip.

However, another locust piercing through the African society and establishing problems for man, thereby depriving him certain rights, is the issue of religious bigotry and cultural diversity. It is clear like the daylight that Africa is a compound of multiple ethnic groups giving rise to diverse culture and religion. The true fact is that no ethnic group is ready to drop or denounce his for the other, and as such, holds it so supreme. This has created hatred and disunity among the citizens of that particular nation. For instance, in Nigeria, which made up of many ethnic groups but recognizes only the three major ones—Igbo, Hausa and Yoruba; an Igbo man cannot exercise his right of peacefully acquiring land and living happily because of religious and cultural diversity. A firm headed by a Hausa man cannot employ a Yoruba or Igbo indigene, merely because he is not from his area. Even in admission seeking into federal and state universities, there is segregation and abuse of individual rights, the right or freedom of association. The aftermath of these acts has given rise to limiting the individuals' rights and restricting man to dwell only in his ethnic enclave instead of exploring the nation.

In Nigeria, the feminine gender is regarded frivolously and accorded little or no respect, because they are considered as the weaker sex; therefore they are treated so poorly and deprived of their rights. Although, the girl child is created as a helper to the man, according to the Christian doctrine, the rate at which they are belittled and dehumanized has created a negative picture and is wholly injurious to their image. For instance, they female folk is not granted prestigious positions in the society, they are deprived of family inheritance, but remain victims of the numerous domestic violence and the countless sexual assault stories which have become the order of the day. To my best understanding, rape is a forceful sexual intercourse or assault which is morally degrading. This assault has been on the increase and as such, has become like a wound on one's fingertip that cannot be ignored. Every day on our streets, the girl child is sexually molested and her sacred forest desecrated. This has left them living in terror and their lives dangerously insecure. The aftermath of this is that most of them relive these traumatic experiences in their minds and entertain suicidal thoughts while some have been killed in the process of raping them.

Furthermore, racial discrimination, no doubt has drawn a big line between people of the same nation or continent. It has placed the oppressed group at the lower class of the society and subsequently threw their rights into the dirty gutter. Racial discrimination is the segregation and separation of people of the same nation due to colour differences. For instance, a flashback to the period of Apartheid Regime in South Africa which is still obtainable now is a clear but atrocious act of racial discrimination. The Black South Africans are marginalized, maltreated and their Human Rights abused. In fact, they were ghostly living in a land they are now afraid and devastated to call their own. No right to live, to work or to express themselves. All these caused by mere difference in colour. Where then is the joy of living if rights which are essential ingredients of life are not exercised.In conclusion, even though the dreaded locust has for ages continued to walk through the open street of our dear Africa, there is this premonition and high optimism that if hands are collectively put on deck in redressing and amending these individual and most importantly our political follies, the walking locust could soon grumble and die.

INNOCENT CHIEMEZIE OHAEKWE is a student of English and Literary Studies at the University of Nigeria Nsukka, Alvan Campus Owerri. He is a fast growing writer who wrote basically prose, short stories, poems and essays. He has been published in different anthologies, which include Fifth Chinua Achebe Poetry/Essay Anthology, through which he obtained a certificate as one of the most outstanding authors among fifty others from different countries of the world. Ohaekwe hails from Urualla in Imo State, Nigeria.

AFRICA'S DEVELOPMENT IN THE FACE OF POOR RESPECT FOR HUMAN RIGHTS

GRACE OLUKOYA

Africa performs poorly in the global community when it comes to the issue of human rights protection across board. And this is the same story from one government to another in which force and power are wielded against the citizens of a state. The use of state weapons and policies to terrorise and infringe on the due legal privileges of citizens is so common. In fact, without their use, it is hard for an insider or outsider to recognize when the state crosses the bounds of the law on an individual's rights. Such measures always have specific groups of target—the media personnel, lawyers, activists, political opponents and even dissidents. All these groups of people and more are not spared the inhuman treatment by a government of which they are citizens.

Sometimes, this does not even take the form of a violent expression to be immediately deemed human rights abuses. Failure by government to provide the basics of amenities at any time and place is still considered a rights violation. The definition of human rights refers to those qualities and privileges bestowed on a person which are neither amenable nor can be withdrawn; and are necessary for the full dignity and complete expression of a human. So a lack of basic governmental provision from adequate security to challenges of food and job insecurity all fall under a violation of the basics of human rights. So many countries in Africa unfortunately fall into this category, for where cases of press limitation, political and civil restrictions and such like may not be in the forefront, the absence of government in service delivery is simply distressing. It borders on the alienation of the individual who is a citizen of the state.

Why is there a high incidence of violations perpetrated by state actors against the ordinary people of the state? Often it is for those in power to necessitate total and absolute control over the actions, mind and will of the people. The system of democracy often fails in such countries due to the pre- modern era of many of these countries. Influences such as religion, tradition and culture have a significant influence on how leaders and the governed interact. It is a commonly held belief that leaders are representatives of the Almighty and as such can do and undo according to their wishes. Therefore, many of these nations have little or no understanding of what it means to be a democratic state or claim that reference. The rights and privileges of the citizenry must be duly appreciated and where bigot leaders brazenly violate such rights it is a step towards disaster. Not only for the state but also for the individual; for, what happens eventually is a regression in national development, together with the ever increasing risk of a revolution that may even disintegrate the state.

One may then wonder what is at stake if this trend continues. A lot I would say. What happens to the person who finds himself accused of a crime he did not commit, just because he is perceived to be a threat to the government of the day; or a press member who seeks to tell the story as it is, regardless of who in high positions is shown in evil light; or the jobless man or woman who can't make a sustainable living because of the hardships imposed by government. These people and others like them lose faith in the government and the state. If they wish to vent out their frustrations they become the originators of an unpleasant uprising.

On the other hand, if they are docile but very ambitious they form the continuing support of a tyrannical system so long as they gain something from it. This and many other examples do portray the bleak situation we as Africans find ourselves in. And the truth be told, every country in Africa has a human rights menace, whether it's political and civil rights restrictions or cultural, social and economic rights curtailment. And it's rather a pity that fifty years and more since the independence events of the mid 1900's we are currently worse off overall than at that period. Unemployment, infrastructural decay, unstable polity, absence of effective and essential government services, and political instabilities that metamorphose into civil wars are characteristics of our current situation.

Gone are the days and era when it was highly recommended that African leaders should be persuaded to respect citizens' rights. For the last seventy to hundred years this has been ongoing with little or no hope of it abating. Some despotic Presidents and Heads of State have made it clear they won't back down from their aims and policies. What is then to be done to save Africa from this hopelessness pit of imminent self-destruction? I strongly believe it lies on the youth, the young generation, to rise up as leaders collectively with a single mandate—the mandate to create a better circumstance for themselves, to provide a glorious future for succeeding generations—future where all sound values and principles are upheld and honoured; where functional governments are in place and effective in their duties.

The protection of human rights by the government of a state

provides a common arena for all to be engaged in the development and growth of a country. Africa needs leaders who are forward-thinking and skilful enough to surmount the ever increasing challenges that the continent as a whole faces. This age of extreme knowledge expansion and connectivity provides ample opportunity for the youth to come together against all odds—the odds of suppression, marginalisation, censorship and limited opportunities for growth in the public space. Imagine the results of communal collaboration in ensuring that the marginalized and neglected in our communities are well taken care of. Sometimes, thinking out of the box gives us the chance to realize that together we as a people can achieve a lot even without government assistance. This really may not be a novel idea but it seems that few ever take advantage of this power.

The future of Africa rests in a dynamic and reasonable leadership. Where our current crop of leaders has failed us was basically in not respecting and responding to the wishes of the masses. And where such a culture slowly develops in the corridors of power, it is almost always impossible to remove. Many of these leaders arose at a young age, had revolutionary ideas that were sound, yet the simple things of carrying along the ordinary people in their goals were lacking. In the end, an environment of mistrust is built which is very difficult to clear out. I strongly believe that now is the time for a strong, new and vibrant generation to arise and take on the reins of power and effectively govern in a productive manner.

GRACE OLUKOYA *writes from Taraba State, Nigeria.*

THE ABUSE AND VIOLATIONS OF HUMAN RIGHTS IN AFRICA

GODSTIME NWAEZE

The violations of human rights are unarguably, one of the greatest challenges being experienced through the streets of Lekki and Kankara in Nigeria, Cabo Delgado in Mozambique, Kigali in Rwanda, to Sydenham in South Africa, and indeed across Africa. "In fact, the history of entrenched human rights abuse has been going on for so long that the citizens themselves and the leaders of these countries might not be able to take any action," observed Carine Kaneza Nantulya, the Director of Advocacy, International Human Rights Watch, Africa. Wikipedia defines rights as legal, social, or ethical principles of freedom or entitlement. It goes further to explain human rights as Moral principles or norms that describe certain standards of human behaviour and are regularly protected in municipal and international law. It is universal, inalienable and inherent regardless of age, location, language, religion, or any other status. These rights include, but are not limited to life, security, freedom of expression and association.

In the words of Ramsey Clark, A right is not what someone gives to you; it is what no one can take from you. Little wonder Nelson Mandela opined, To deny people their human rights is to challenge their very humanity. And like many other activists throughout history, he equally dedicated his life to the struggle for human rights. Therefore, human rights abuse entails denying a person any of the rights as provided by necessary legal instruments. In the disposition of Malala Yousafzai who declared that, one child, one teacher, one book, one pen can change the world, this essay therefore, seeks to highlight the violations of human rights in Africa and its causes, and proffer noteworthy recommendations.

THE LEGAL EFFECT OF HUMAN RIGHTS ABUSE IN AFRICA

There are different legal instruments that have been put in place to secure human rights regionally and in individual states. These notwithstanding, violations have sadly been persistent. The fourth article of Part one of the African Charter on Human and Peoples' Rights expressly states that human beings are inviolable. Every human being shall be entitled to respect for his life and the integrity of his person. No one may be arbitrarily deprived of this right.

In Section 34(1) of the Constitution of the Federal Republic of Nigeria, it declares thus, Every person is entitled to respect for the dignity of his person. The ECOWAS Community Court of Justice on March 18, 2015, withdrew the restrictions on freedom of expression placed on the plaintiff in the case of Ogwuche vs. Federal Republic of Nigeria. Consequent upon these, the law also enshrines duties and obligations which everyone is bound to uphold, and their breach constitutes human rights abuse. It is pertinent to note that the State has the responsibility to safeguard human rights, and in effect, it suffices to say that these violations are caused by the State directly, through wrongful use of its police force, or indirectly when it fails to provide fundamental needs leading to abuse or death.

INSTANCES OF HUMAN RIGHTS ABUSE IN AFRICA

The sacredness of human life in Nigeria has almost lost its meaning. In 2009, Amnesty International published an article entitled, 'Killings at Will: Extra-judicial Executions and Other Unlawful Killing by the Police in Nigeria'; and it reported thirty-nine cases of security force killings and enforced disappearances. Presently, there are incessant abductions of students; there have been Chibok girls, Kankara and Kagara abductions. We have also witnessed the protest calling for an end to police brutality by the defunct department of the Nigerian police, Special Anti-Robbery Squad, which allegedly masterminded the death of many innocent Nigerians. Jimoh Isiaq, for one, was shot dead during the protest. Worst still, Boko Haram is in its eleventh year, and has continued to kill at will. In Nigeria, freedom after speech is not guaranteed.

Similarly, xenophobic attack leading to scores of death, displacement, and intrusion of personal liberty in South Africa is no longer news, and South Africa has been criticized on the ground that virtually no one has been convicted of recent or past xenophobic violence.

Elsewhere, human rights record in Tanzania has continued to deteriorate. The media and government critics [are] restricted, civil society groups deregistered, and the rights of women and children, undermined.

Rwanda, Burundi, Guinea, Uganda and many African countries are not left out. The governments are not willingly democratic; they clamp down protests and dissents, political and student rallies are banned, and political opponents are arrested. Central African Republic continues to be one of the most dangerous countries in the world for humanitarian actors.

THE CAUSES OF HUMAN RIGHTS ABUSE IN AFRICA

Poor administration of justice: The administration of justice is the cornerstone of every democratic State upon which the structure of civil society is built, and the absence of truly independent judiciary in many African countries serves as one of the root causes of human rights violations. Interestingly, a writer rightly observed that, "Without justice, life would not be possible, and even if it were, it would not be worth living." In many neighbourhoods in Nigeria, there is careless and rampant abuse of human rights. Worst still, the perpetrators of these inhuman acts are rarely brought to book; and while the judiciary bootlicks the executive, the latter continues to carry out undemocratic acts against the people without accountability. Justice has become a commodity bought by the highest bidder.

• *Poverty and ignorance.* It is true that poverty is ravaging many parts of Africa despite her endowments, and this in itself, is an abuse of right to livelihood occasioned by excessive looting. Consequently, people sell their basic rights for a day's lunch. Others give up their rights as they may be powerless to fight these negative forces, due to their low social status. On the other hand, owing to illiteracy, many people do not know their human rights, let alone demand for their enforcement. Thus, they are left at the mercy of careless violators. Indeed, Frederick Douglas was right when he said "Knowledge makes a man unfit to be a slave."

• *The autocratic nature of leadership in Africa.* There is no gainsaying that most leaders in Africa are willing to cling to power even at the expense of the people. As a result, they engage in gross violations of human rights just to remain in power and wield sovereignty. This is evident during elections when there is usually abuse of freedom of speech, killings and unwarranted arrests. In the modern time, Goodluck Ebele Jonathan stands out as a model, on the contrary.

• *Ethnic rivalry.* The hostility ensuing between different ethnicities in Nigeria, for instance, has caused colossal infringement of human rights in many forms, such as murder, rape and destruction of personal property. The havoc orchestrated by the Fulani herdsmen is considered to have ethnic undertone. In the circumstance, there is a proscribed outfit called Eastern Security Network, formed by Nnamdi Kanu, the leader of the Independent People of Biafra; and the concern is that these ethnic strives heighten the violations of human rights.

• *Corruption and press dependency.* Corruption is a distinctive feature of politics in Africa, and according to Professor Peter U. Nwangwu, Corruption is potent cancer that has mercilessly eaten Nigeria to a state of stupor. Its end products range from embezzlement, deprivation of social and economic rights, and dependency of the press. In Nigeria for example, the Nigerian Television Authority, which is the mainstream media did not report the events of Lekki Toll Gate during the protests against Police brutality. All these undermine human rights.

RECOMMENDATIONS

• Effective international watchdog and strict sanctions for States that violate human rights.
• Increased struggle by human rights activists and institutions against abuses.
• Harmonization of conflicting interests between tribes.
• Independent judiciary, and initiating civil actions rather

than resorting to self-help.
- Mass enlightenment campaign and political participation.

CONCLUSION

Human rights are God-given, and are the same for every person at all times; as such, if we must continue to live together, the protection of these rights is not negotiable. The African States must resolve to tackle this pandemic by willingness to give democracy its truest expression, and the provision of basic needs which amplify the human dignity. In the same vein, human rights organizations and indeed, everyone must seek to respect and promote our common human rights. It is what makes us human.

GODSTIME NWAEZE *is a Nigerian writer who hails from Izzi in Ebonyi State, Nigeria. He is presently studying Law at Nnamdi Azikiwe University, Awka, Anambra State, from where he writes.*

HUMAN RIGHTS ABUSE AND VIOLATIONS IN AFRICA

FRANKLIN IFEANYI DIALA

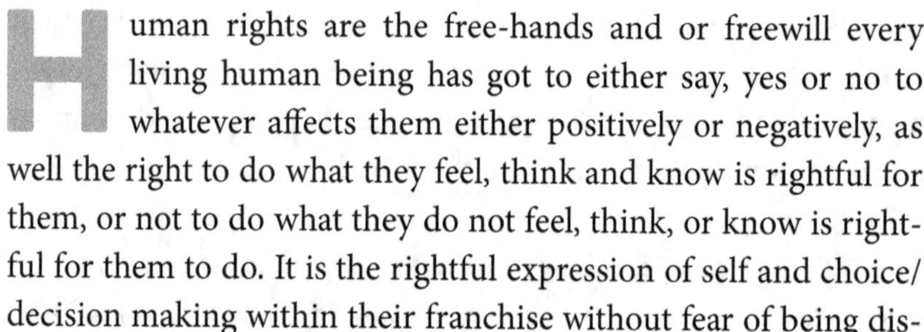

Human rights are the free-hands and or freewill every living human being has got to either say, yes or no to whatever affects them either positively or negatively, as well the right to do what they feel, think and know is rightful for them, or not to do what they do not feel, think, or know is rightful for them to do. It is the rightful expression of self and choice/decision making within their franchise without fear of being discriminated, stigmatized, battered or imprisoned.

When those rights aren't protected or blatantly disregarded, they are abused and violated.

Our African human rights seem to have become privileges rather than rights. It is being abused and violated. The right to freely express self, thoughts, and publicly speak against societal ills such as: bad leadership, injustice, intimidation, oppression, negative religious influence, wrong orientation on race, ethnicism and tribalism, impunity and corruption, has been deprived via limitation and imposition of certain measures by the government, traditional rulers, community heads, family head, etc.

The measures have inhibited freedom of speech and expression, allowed coercion (using force to make people do what is not right for selfish interest), political intimidation and oppression, as well from elites (wealthy bad eggs). Other factors include, bad influence, peer pressure, poor upbringing from a bad home (not to forget that a child's training starts from the home), poor educational background, ignorance etc. The contributing factors, as mentioned above, have actually led to the abuse and violation of human rights in Africa.

Human rights abuse and violations that are common in Africa are: gross domestic violence (especially against women) and rape, sexual abuse (even in marital homes), child abuse (as can be seen in child hawking, child trafficking, child slavery and teenage marriage), also religious bigotry, racial discrimination, ethnicism, tribalism, human trafficking, prohibition/limitation of same sex activities, limitation to freedom of assembly and association (especially one that is targeted towards societal and governmental ills), monopoly of power, unauthorized intrusion of privacy, restriction of press freedom, corruption of government officials, impunity, absence of independence and neutrality in the judiciary, rigging of elections, limitation/prohibition of voting right, delay or refusal to pay workers salary/wages as and when due, kidnapping, extrajudicial killings, enforced disappearance and torture, limitation to sexual lifestyle, forced marriages, forced abortions, prisoner abuse, police brutality, political oppression and repression, religious persecution, infringement of right to fair trial, insecurity, lynching, etc, to mention but a few. Let's talk about few:

GROSS DOMESTIC VIOLENCE

This is considered as the most common of human rights violation in Africa. Here the man of the house/husband, violently abuses his wife, child or children and the maid. Domestic violence is not only inflicted by men, as most women are known to have domestically maltreated their wards/maids. In other words, there are some men who are domestically violated too.

This could come as brutality (merciless beating, punching, and flogging) rape or sexual abuse. It applies to both men/boy, women/girl, but it is the girl child or women who suffers domestic violence the most. In most cases, they are sternly warned not to tell anyone about it or risk their lives.

CHILD ABUSE

This is a common violation of rights, where a child (boy or girl) is being misused/abused. Children are being taken into slavery, drug trafficking, prostitution, teenage/forced marriage, they are being trafficked, sexually abused, and used to hawk. I see this as the highest form of abuse and violation among others because children are the future of tomorrow and the mentality of tomorrow's future is being toiled with and deformed.

These children pass through lots of pains growing up and this makes them tough in the negative, thereby causing restiveness in their societies/communities due to their engaging in various criminal acts which affects the society at large. The girls are mostly sexually abused and forced into teenage marriage as well sex addicts, while the boys become drug addicts, thugs and armed robbers. If this should continue to happen, the African future might be damned.

IMPUNITY

In a country or society where anybody, especially those in power, can get away with whatever ills committed against humanity or the vulnerable humans, that country/society has failed to protect the rights of her citizen and has contributed to their human rights violation. For instance in some African countries, a policeman can beat up an innocent fellow citizen (who is supposed to be under his protection), and say to himself and to the citizen, Nothing will happen even if I should kill you here and he gets away with it. A politician could violently deprive citizens the right to vote and get away with the mind inscription that nothing will happen. Also, a man could turn his wife into a regular punching bag and still gets away with it. I have experienced a scenario where a woman was threatened with a knife and robbed in broad day light, and people who could have helped turned a blind eye. They were seeing it happen but could not go close to help because they were afraid to be the next victim of circumstance, and nobody would say anything. Impunity!

RACIAL DISCRIMINATION

A good example of this abuse and violation of rights was seen in the xenophobic attack of South Africans against Nigerians living in South Africa. Vulnerable Nigerians were attacked and some were killed in the attack and their rights to be among their South African family as well run their usual day-to-day activities/business, were all of a sudden infringed on, due to racial discrimination. Perhaps something or someone might have influenced that racial move by South Africans to have thought of depriving Nigerians in South African the right to live among them.

TRIBALISM, ETHNICISM AND RELIGIOUS BIGOTRY

When tribalism, religious fanaticism, and ethicism become the case in an African country/state with different religious groups, there tend to be abuse and violation of religious rights. Where one religious group sees herself as the only one true religion and then discriminates others on the basis of their religion or tribe, then religious or tribalistic violence is inevitable. Human rights have been violated, and crisis may abound. In an African state/country with diverse religious groups, no particular religion should have the monopoly of power, or else there will be political clash and might lead to subsequent full-blown war.

LIMITATION TO VOTING

Voting is a fundamental human right. Every citizen of an African country/state should have the right to vote and be voted for as and when due. There should be no limitation to voting. If these should be, then it becomes an abuse and violation of a fundamental human right.

DELAY OR REFUSAL TO PAY WAGES/SALARY

Every worker has the right to their wages/salary and as when due. If an employer fails to pay the salary of his/her worker at the right time, then it is an infringement of human right; it is a violation of right. Violation can either be intentionally performed by a state, country or an individual failing to prevent the violation.

Violation can be physically violent in nature as in the case of police brutality, gross domestic violence and rape, extrajudicial killings, torture, forced abortion, etc, while rights such as the right to fair trial can be violated, where no physical violence is involved. Also, when there is a conflict between individuals or groups within a society, if the state does nothing to intervene and protect vulnerable people and groups it is participating in the violations.

It is on this note that I crave our indulgence, especially as Africans, to put a halt to the abuse and violations of human rights in Africa by intervening and protecting/securing the human rights and lives of Africans, especially those of the vulnerable. Africans' lives matter.

FRANKLIN IFEANYI DIALA *is a native of Obodo Owu-Amakohia autonomous community, Ikdeuru L.G.A. of Imo State, Nigeria. He is a graduate of Microbiology from Imo State University, Owerri. He is also an essayist, a creative non-fiction writer and a poet.*

HUMAN RIGHTS ABUSE AND VIOLATIONS IN AFRICA

FLOSSY KAMBUKU

Nelson Mandela once said, To deny people of their human rights is to challenge their very humanity. These are rights everyone has, and everyone equally by virtue of their very humanity. All people regardless of their race, skin color, religious beliefs, sex, sexual preferences and abilities are entitled to their rights by the time they are born. These rights can only survive under a system of law and that is why the United Nations General Assembly adopted on, 10th December 1948, a universal declaration of human rights. The fact that the idea of human rights was declared universal did not and does not until now stop some individuals from infringing inhumane actions on other people and this is what is called human rights abuse and violation. This essay discusses human rights abuses and violations in Africa like the abuse of the rights of detainees, female genital mutilation, and the abuse of rights of workers.

To begin with, some examples of human rights are; right to life, right of detained persons to be treated with humanity, right to fair trial, right to just and favorable conditions of work, right to health, right to education and right to privacy. Sadly, most people are not aware that they have these rights. African countries adopted democracy which requires the respect of human rights although it is so on paper only. Africa's poor human rights record is caused by racism, post-colonialism, ignorance, diseases, religious intolerance, internal conflicts, debts, bad management, corruption, the monopoly of power, lack of judicial and press autonomy, border conflicts and poverty which is a dominant factor. More than seventy-five percent of the continent's 700 million people live below the poverty line, and ten of the world's thirteen poorest countries are in Africa. People would rather have their rights violated or receive bad treatment as long as they get money or food in return.

Secondly, detainees have the right to be treated with humanity; they are also people after all. They have the right to fair trial but this is not what is happening on ground in African prisons and jails. Most of the human rights issues that detainees in African countries for example in Malawi go through include: extrajudicial killings, torture, arbitrary detention, the preceding abuses all committed by official security forces; harsh and life-threatening prison and detention center conditions. The fact that these people committed crime does not mean that they deserve to live in places of poor sanitation; with no toilets, poorly prepared food, and poor medical attention. The law also provides detainees the right to have access to legal counsel and be released from detention or informed of charges within 48 hours of arrest; however, authorities often ignore these rights. The police frequently demand bribes to authorize bail, which is often granted to reduce overcrowding in jails, rather than release a detainee on the merits of a case. Detainees' relatives are sometimes denied access to them. The judicial system, even though they are aware of these violations, does nothing about it because they are handicapped by serious weaknesses including poor record keeping, heavy caseloads and corruption.

In continuation, police sometimes use excessive torture to silence or interrogate detainees, which sometimes leads to the deaths of some. This is an abuse and violation of human rights. Perpetrators of such abuses are occasionally punished administratively like transferring them to another police unit but investigations often are delayed or abandoned. These types of punishments do not help in reducing the abuse of human rights rather they only increase and change the location of the abuse. The situation is also not changing because of ignorance and fear of the detainees. Some of the detainees may not have any idea that their rights are being violated and those who know fear to report the police to higher officials and suffer in silence. Sensitization on human rights and their violation punishments in prisons and jails will save detainees from falling victim to these abuses.

Furthermore, another example of human rights violation and abuse activity that this essay will tackle is Female Genital Mutilation (FGM). Female genital mutilation involves the forced removal of part or all the female genitalia against one's will. African countries like Kenya, Somalia, Ethiopia, Tanzania and Uganda have millions of girls and women that have experienced FGM. In Kenya, overall 21% of girls and women have undergone this traumatizing practice varying from 98% in the north eastern region to 1% in the western region. Girls and women from rural areas, living in poor households, with less education or who identify as Muslim are the ones that likely to fall victims of FGM. Medical personnel with all their knowledge sometimes are also responsible for the practice, especially among the Kissi in Kenya. The question might be, If medical personnel are doing that to the helpless women and girls, then, who is to sensitize and protect helpless girls against FGM? Most regions in Kenya have achieved progress towards eliminating FGM which is promising, in the north eastern region however the practice still remains universal. Women and girls whose rights have been violated in this way face many health issues during sexual intercourse or giving birth and they get blamed by their partners, as if it was their fault. They need a strong voice to speak on their behalf and save the future generation from FGM. That is why girls and women need to be sensitized of the negatives of FGM and where they can report such practices. There is power in information.

Lastly, the last human rights abuse act that this essay will cover is the abuse of rights of workers. The law prohibits all forms of compulsory or forced labor and allows for the right to just and favorable work conditions. These are not always respected. Workers, particularly in industrial jobs, often work without safety equipment and clothing; for example: facemasks, gloves and overalls. In tobacco fields workers harvesting leaves generally do not wear protective clothing; workers absorb up to 54 milligrams of dissolved nicotine daily through their skin, the equivalent of 50 cigarettes. In other industries, the chemicals that workers absorb have everlasting side effects; for example, skin cancer, which they deal with on their own without any help or compassion from their employers. Workers also receive salaries which are below the minimum wage just because the owners of the industries want to make profits. As if the low wages are not enough damage, workers are given late/delayed pay even though they are overworked. They work extra hours and get done in one day the work that was supposed to be for two or three days. Workers have the right to remove themselves from dangerous work situations without jeopardy to continued employment. Workers dismissed for filing complaints regarding workplace conditions have the right to file a complaint at the labor office or sue the employer for wrongful dismissal; however, due to ignorance of such rights and high levels of unemployment, workers are unlikely to exercise these rights. Additionally, authorities do not effectively protect employees in this situation yet they want a productive nation.

In conclusion, all human rights abuse and violations in Africa can be reduced to even 0% if high authorities pay more attention to victims and violators. Victims and everyone else need to be educated on their rights and where to report if their rights have been violated. Introducing human rights as a subject in junior levels in schools can be better than only having the constitution. All people who abuse human rights should be punished accordingly. It is possible to have an Africa free from human rights abuse and violations.

FLOSSY KAMBUKU *writes from Malawi.*

TEENAGE SEXUAL MOLESTATION: RETHINKING THE HAVOC ON THE GIRL CHILD

CHARLES IORNUMBE

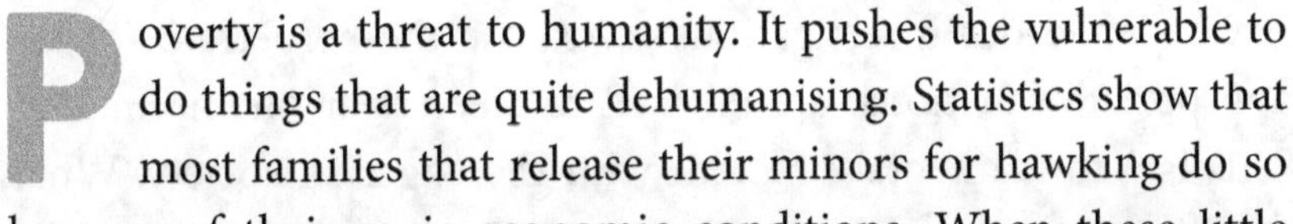

Poverty is a threat to humanity. It pushes the vulnerable to do things that are quite dehumanising. Statistics show that most families that release their minors for hawking do so because of their socio-economic conditions. When these little ones are sent out, they are exposed to various forms of danger such as molestation and sexual abuse.

In Nigeria today, no fewer than three cases of child sexual abuse are reported every week in some communities. Some other cases are not known because access to such information is difficult. It is appalling to note that most families have mortgaged the comfort of their children especially the girl child for petty trading as part of the daily efforts to put food on their tables. To such children, their education does not matter. This is because the resources to send them to school to acquire western education like other children from well-to-do families are simply not there.

Now, the concern here is the dangers the female child faces when forced to go out in the streets to hawk. First, she is likely to be molested and sexually abused. These children come from homes that are so much disadvantaged and at the merest chance where they are lured for money, food and drinks, they easily fall victim. Some very disturbing scenarios play out where a teenager is raped and deflowered, thus, violating her rights as a human being. The parents of the rape survivor usually don't want the criminality exposed. This is probably for the fear of stigmatisation and the toga of shame the child might carry into adulthood.

Most people believe that the survivor might also have it tough getting a spouse. The parents, for these reasons, prefer to meet with the perpetrator of the crime to settle the matter without much interference. When this happens, security agencies, Non-Governmental Organisations, NGOs, and media professionals that could have carried out investigations to expose the perpetrator(s) for appropriate sanctions, are advised to steer clear off the matter. This is a fundamental problem with the Nigerian society. What families of the rape survivor fail to realise is that, they leave the girls to suffer the traumatic pains inflicted on them. The teenager lives not only to be wary of every male around but also hates to see men.

Few months ago, two young men were reported to have approached a journalist with a report of an over sixty-year-old man raping a less than ten year-old-girl who was sent out hawking. As a journalist, he quickly commenced investigation only to find out that a relation of the minor had connived with an elder in the community to conceal the crime. His findings confirmed the allegation that money had exchanged hands. When the man under whose roof the teenage girl was staying wanted to follow up on the matter, he was frustrated on claims that he only married the girl's mother and should not be involved in the affairs of a child he is not the father. To further investigate the matter, the journalist approached some relevant security experts including the police and National Agency for the Prohibition of Trafficking in Persons (NAPTIP). A NAPTIP official reportedly told the journalist that if the matter were reported to their office on the spot, it could have been easier for them to take action. He said they could have examined the rape survivor to ascertain whether or not she was penetrated.

A police officer advised the journalist on telephone to find out whether or not the family would like to pursue the matter further before taking action to avoid a court case. He contacted the family members of the victim who appealed that he should not go on with investigation—that they had scheduled a family meeting to resolve the matter. According to the newsman, his investigation stalled for these reasons leaving his heart with a huge moral ache.

What is painful is that we live to see perpetrators of this type of crime go about freely. If you check out, families of the teenagers affected don't even take the survivors to nearby medical facilities for thorough check up to ascertain their health conditions. What if minors raped develop complications which might worsen in future? Will their families feel the pinch of what they had allowed or share in the woes? Will the survivors forgive anyone and forget when they eventually grow up to know their stories? And what do you think they could do to help themselves? These are possible questions borne of out a genuine concern that Nigerians must ponder on and evolve a workable solution. Now, if you put yourself in the shoes of one who is being raped, how does it feel? Or as a 'no nonsense' parent whose child has suffered such a fate, what will be your reaction? It is common to hear that men rape minors for ritual purposes. If this is true, one would say, it is devilish, and an act of man's inhumanity to man.

Government has a huge task here. It must consciously set out to mete out appropriate punitive measures against perpetrators of rape. Government must also be ready to bring families of those raped to book with equally appropriate legal frameworks if they try to shield perpetrators. This is against the backdrop of the fact that, the family is at the centre of every incident of child rape. Communities where such acts are committed must rise to protest such evil. These will eliminate the fear of possible litigation by families against individuals and bodies such as the media and Non-Governmental Organizations with the intention to expose the criminality.

The girl child is so precious that we all must continue to protect her hence the adage that when you train a woman, it is the whole nation.

Have we not read or heard of how influential educated and well-informed women in the society have been and even contributed to nation building? Think about the late professor Dora Akunyili the former DG of NAFDAC in Nigeria, Ellen Johnson Sirleaf former Sierra Leone President, Margaret Thatcher former British Prime Minister, Dr. Ngozi Okonjo-Iweala the current Director General of World Trade Organisation WTO, Dr. Obi Ezekwesili, former minister of Education, Chief Mrs. Margaret Icheen of Benue who became the first female speaker of the State House of Assembly in West Africa, Princess Countess of Snowdon and Margaret Ekpo a foremost Nigerian Politician just to mention but a few. Just any girl could be like any of such great women. So why would anyone like to destroy the future of the girl child for ritual purposes? Rapists ought to be made to face the full wrath of the law after which they should repent and seek restitution for God to forgive them otherwise they may be doomed forever.

CHARLES IORNUMBE *works at the Directorate of News & Current Affairs, Radio Benue Corporation, Makurdi, Benue State.*

THE STREETS OF LAW PROSTITUTION IN AFRICA AND THE QUEST FOR HUMAN DIGNITY

BONFACE ISABOKE NYAMWEYA

Better laws, as better nations, are what humanity desires and deserves. Whenever there are good laws, normally, there is order. Whenever there is order, there are good laws. The goodness of the laws sprouts from their capacity to foster the realisation of people's deep ambitions. When a people will prosperity, peace, and harmony, they will, at the same time, the essence of particular laws that can secure the fruition of such noble ambitions. This means that a people with good ambitions ought to decoct their success in a path of laws sprinkled with indigenous goodwill.

However, we learn from experience that it is not just about having good laws, rather being conscious that such laws are not something alien to us. African nations face today a lot of violation of human rights, not because we lack laws protecting human rights, but especially because of alienation. The laws in our constitutions and the laws enacted by the International Community are mostly attributed to Western Jurisprudence. Although African Jurisprudence is given some platform, nonetheless, it is rendered as inferior by the assumption that it is not codified. Consequently, such alienates the Africans in their societies since they do not feel the indigenous goodwill as part of their aspirations, whenever such laws are invoked.

THE GRAND PREJUDICE

It is sincere to note that African Jurisprudence is not only present in the African Customary laws, rather in each formulation of laws where the Africans are involved. To attribute the idea of human rights primarily to Western Jurisprudence is just to broadcast lies. This is because in the African communities, even before colonization, each African culture had a unique way of expressing respect to each other and even the reverence of life.

One may argue that most African cultures looked down upon women and children, while over-glorifying the male persons. Strictly, each culture is in a continuous flux. Thus, African cultures are not immune of the paradigm shift. Our approach to women and children has been modified by our new awareness that they too deserve to be treated as full human persons. We know that even in the United Kingdom, women initially were not allowed to vote. This means that the evolution of our laws is spontaneous in each culture due to our change of perception as our understanding changes with time.

We cannot take kindly therefore, the idea that human rights are a comparatively recent phenomenon in Africa. African Customary law, to a great extent is not codified. Yet, those to whom it applies understand its provisions on human rights. Above all, the participation of Africans in the International Community must not be taken as insignificant. When we take part in the enactment of laws in the United Nations for instance, we actively air our suggestions there. Since our suggestions carry our aspirations as a people, our culture is represented there. To this extent therefore, African Customary law is broadcast even in International Laws where Africans participate.

ALIENATION AS THE ROOT OF HUMAN RIGHTS VIOLATION IN AFRICA

The sphere of influence of each nation is directly proportional to her capacity to dictate directly or indirectly the laws to be used by herself and some of her neighbours. The power of influence flows from culture, politics, and such other categories of practical importance. All these categories gleam the kind of laws we develop as a nation. As before, we observe that weaker nations are shaped into the legal systems designed for them by the powerful nations, directly or indirectly.

Peering into the iridescent mirror of history, it is evident that Africa was once colonised. Before colonialism, the African people had their ways of settling disputes. Civil and criminal liabilities were not lacking in African societies. The coming of the white man brought a new texture of jurisprudence, but it is not true that the white man brought the entirety of jurisprudence to Africa. Instead, the interaction of the Africans with the whites has gradually yielded to a hybrid of jurisprudence. Both Western Jurisprudence and African Jurisprudence supplement each other.

Jean-Paul Sartre, in his preface to Frantz Fanon's Wretched of the Earth notes that, We know it is not a uniform world, and it still contains subjected peoples, some of whom have acquired a false independence, others who are fighting to conquer their sovereignty, and yet others who have won their freedom, but who live under the constant threat of imperialist aggression. Although African countries gained their independence, it seems they lost it immediately to their own hands.

Neo-colonialism is the new form of colonialism. Africa is split by her own leaders. Fanon cautions that, The colonial world is a compartmentalized world. We do experience today sanctions being issued by stronger nations against weaker African nations who refuse to comply with the dictates made. Our African political leaders therefore execute neo-colonialism because the colonizer still lives and has an insatiable appetite to indirectly dominate our projects, our everything basically.

It is interesting that forty or thirty years from independence, many African communities are still looking for their way forward, with a new identity and new values. The quest for a new constitution, a new-found democracy and a market economy of their own are the driving force in most post-colonial African countries.

Since our leaders lack autonomy to execute our African goodwill, most of our African countries are especially identified with a high voltage of corruption, racial discrimination, monopoly of power, suffocation of judicial and press autonomy, unauthorized intrusion of privacy, debt and bad financial management. Our African countries have become the streets of law prostitution breeding injustice; whereby, laws are forced to justify injustices done to innocent citizens by those in power.

THE WAY FORWARD

To this far, we need something beyond the laws. We need something to awaken the vivacity of our African spirit to work as a family wherefrom we derive our purpose and meaning and reciprocate the same to the community. In a way, if we cannot feel being at home, we will remain at the suffering terminal intentioned only for pauperism, war, hatred, corruption, and all forms of violence and violations of human rights.

We may come up with noble laws, but without the link with our communal aspirations as Africans, such will again be manipulated gradually to serve individual gratification or even those who referee our leaders from without. The concept of Ubuntu must smear the cracks of our current situation on human rights violation. This is because Ubuntu is a relational concept, whereby the individual subject derives meaning and purpose for his existence from the community, and in turn gives greater meaning and purpose to the community, (I am because we are; we are because I am).

It is important to highlight that the concept [Ubuntu] includes a code of compassion, which goes beyond the right, the wrong, and the duty. Every activity and involvement of the individual is seen in terms of participation and collaboration in teamwork and in a family spirit. We will therefore be able to see and treat each other as full human persons who deserve care, love and dignity. Our cultural differences, our linguistic backgrounds, our geographical differences, will no longer trigger a feeling of aggression towards one another. The lens of perception will be in terms of one family of a people intentioned to make humanity great. Africa will be identified with progress and mutual respect of other people's rights.

CONCLUSION

It is evident that for dignity to reign in Africa, we must efface the current spirit of alienation. Once we take our laws as our own making, we will be able to execute them in order to realize our aspirations as a people. Africa will no longer be a labyrinth of the streets of law prostitution, rather a place of order, care, love and progress. Therefore, for Africa to step forward, we must feel at home in our matters of practical importance. This is the antidote for our current violations of human rights. It is a clarion call for all of us to join our hands to see this dream realized for Africa.

REFERENCE

• *Frantz Fanon, The Wretched of the Earth, Richard Philcox, trans., Grove Press, New York, 1963.*

• *Stephen Okello, Western Humanism in Dialogue with African Ubuntu for the Greater Good, Ascolto dellAfrica, Urbaniana University Press, Rome, 2012.*

*Born in 1997, **BONFACE ISABOKE NYAMWEYA** is a Kenyan Law student at the University of Nairobi, Parklands. He is also pursuing his Masters in Philosophy at the Catholic University of Eastern Africa. He is the author of "Peeling the Cobwebs", which treats the theme of tribalism in Ricafa, one of the African countries. "Her Question Pills" is his recent novel treating Feminism and African Womanism.*

THE NIGERIA'S CASE

ABDULLATEEF B. ISA

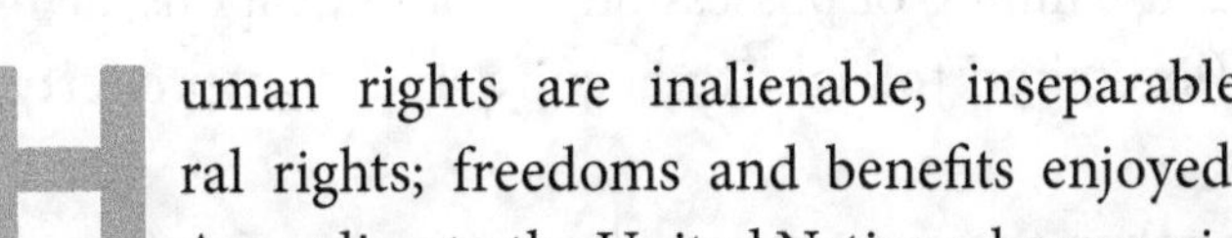

Human rights are inalienable, inseparable, and natural rights; freedoms and benefits enjoyed by humans. According to the United Nations, human rights are rights inherent to all human beings, regardless of race, sex, nationality, ethnicity, language, religion, or any other status. Many documents and laws were enacted in recognition and defence of human rights, among which are the Universal Declaration of Human Rights, 1948; the International Covenant on Civil and Political Rights, 1966; the International Covenant on Economic, Social and Cultural Rights, 1966; the African Charter on Human and People's Rights, 1981; and the Convention on the Rights of the Child, 1989.

At the national level, the Chapter IV (Section 33 to 44) of the 1999 Constitution of the Federal Republic of Nigeria discusses the following fundamental rights: rights to life; right to dignity of human persons; right to personal liberty; right to fair hearing; right to private and family life; right to freedom of thought, conscience and religion; right to freedom of expression and the press; right to peaceful assembly and association; right to freedom of movement; right to freedom from discrimination; right to acquire and own immovable property; and compulsory acquisition of property.

Unfortunately, despite all these laws and documents, human

rights are still abused and violated. Well, we must not forget that there are limitations to certain human rights. Among them are: death sentence (limitation to right to life); convictions, curfew, and restrictions on movement (limitations to right to freedom of movement); laws against slander, libel, and sedition (limitations to right to freedom of expression); proscription on certain groups and secret societies (limitation to right to peaceful assembly and association); and banning of possession of some weapons, arms, ammunition (limitation to right to acquire and own property); among others.

Moving further, the most serious human rights violations in Nigeria currently are done by terrorists, bandits, militants, and killer herdsmen. Their heinous acts result in killings, bombings, forced evictions, mass displacements, and destructions of private and public properties. In an attempt to halt these acts, actions of security forces also result in other sets of human rights violations such as arbitrary arrests, accidental discharges, unjust detentions, killings, and torture.

Police brutality, unlawful bans, use of excessive force, and harassment of activists, peaceful protesters, and political opponents are common instances of human rights abuses. These abuses have denied citizens their civil and political rights. Journalists, investigators and media professionals were not spared too. A recent occurrence was in August 2020 when a former Aviation Minister, Femi Fani-Kayode verbally assaulted a journalist in Calabar, Cross River State. This is a serious abuse of the right to freedom of expression and the journalistic ethics.

Another serious instance of human rights violation is the attack on school children. Education in Nigeria, particularly the Northern Nigeria, is under attack. Between December 2020 and

February 2021, more than three cases of abductions of school children were recorded. On 11th December, 2020, 344 schoolboys were kidnapped at Government Science Secondary School, Kankara, Katsina State. The second abduction took place on February 17, 2021 at Government Science College, Kagara, Niger State, where 42 persons were kidnapped. The third abduction which happened on the 26th of February, 2021, was the abduction of 279 girls from Government Girls Science Secondary School, Jangebe, Zamfara State. Thank God, all the abductees have been freed and united with their families. It was reported that some students have not returned to school due to the attacks, and that may be an end of education of such children.

Child marriage (marriage before the age of 18) is another violation of human rights; but unfortunately, it is prevalent nowadays, most especially, in the Northern Nigeria. Child marriage denies girls their rights, and even drives them into experiences that they lack the capacity to withstand. Child marriage affects male children too. Another violation of child's rights is child labour. Child labour and slavery expose youngsters to hazardous acts that may affect them intellectually, physically, socially, morally, and mentally. It is even likely to interfere with their education and overall development. Other violations of child's rights are child trafficking, child slavery, sexual abuse, excessive beating, child abandonment, street hawking, disregard for persons with disabilities, begging, and using of children for thuggery and hooliganism.

Banning the use of hijab by some educational institutions is a violation of the right of Muslim women to practise their religion. The Universal Declaration of Human Rights (Article 18), the 1999 Nigerian Constitution (Section 38), and other similar human rights instruments allow every person to manifest his religion or belief in teaching, practice, worship and observance, but in many cases, authorities infringe on this fundamental right. Similar to this is the compulsion of (a) religious discipline(s) or practice(s) on students that do not believe in such belief.

Discrimination of persons on the basis of ethnicity, region, and religion is another means of violation of human rights. Many of the killer herdsmen, for example, are known to be Fulanis, so that has given some persons the courage to regard all Fulani herdsmen as killers, and that is wrong, a violation of their rights. Criminalism is not the signature of a particular ethnic or region, and an entire ethnic group shouldn't be characterised with it. As regards religious discrimination, there are instances where persons are molested and humiliated because of their belief or religious practice.

Attack on members of the Nigeria Police Force is another instance of human rights violations. During the October 2020 protests against brutality of the Special Anti-Robbery Squad (SARS) unit of the Nigeria Police Force, some policemen were burnt alive, while some were even eaten after being burnt. We must not forget that those police officers are human beings like us, and that they deserve the respect and dignity we also deserve.

Unfortunately, many cases of human rights abuse and violations did not see justice due to lack or absence of independent and fearless judiciary, and influence of powerful individuals on judicial processes. The Government must hold everyone and even itself accountable and ensure that justice is served. Civil societies also have a role to play in preventing human rights violations. When human rights violations happened, either directly or indirectly, they should speak out and hold violators responsible. The international community too should adequately monitor governments and ensure the upholding, promotion, recognition, and advancement of human rights. Human rights violations are rampant nowadays, and should not be allowed to stay!

ABDULLATEEF B. ISA *is a Motivational Speaker, Writer and Essayist. He writes from Ibadan, the Capital of Oyo State, Nigeria.*

FIFTEEN INSPIRING HUMAN RIGHTS QUOTES

Culled from the official website of the Amnesty International

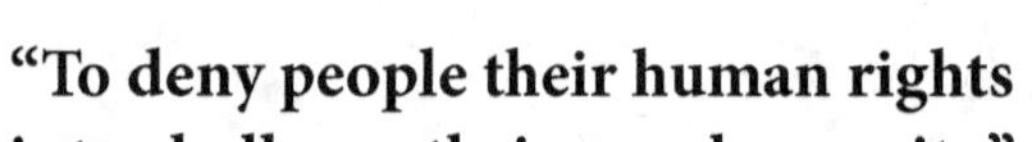

**"To deny people their human rights
is to challenge their very humanity."**
Nelson Mandela, South African civil rights activist

**"Activism works. So what I'm telling you to do now is
to act, because no one is too small to make a difference."**
*Greta Thunberg, Swedish climate change activist and
Amnesty International Ambassador of Conscience*

**"It means a great deal to those who are oppressed to
know that they are not alone. Never let anyone tell you
that what you are doing is insignificant."**
Desmond Tutu, South African civil rights activist

**"If you want to improve your quality of life and
the quality of life for all women, never stop
questioning society or calling for change."**
Justina De Pierris, Argentinian student activist

"Injustice anywhere is a threat to justice everywhere."
Martin Luther King, African-American civil rights activist

"The candle burns not for us, but for all those whom we failed to rescue from prison, who were shot on the way to prison, who were tortured, who were kidnapped, who 'disappeared'. That's what the candle is for."
Peter Benenson, founder of Amnesty International

"Peace can only last where human rights are respected, where the people are fed, and where individuals and nations are free."
14th Dalai Lama, the highest spiritual leader of Tibet and the retired political leader of Tibet

---

"Letters aren't just a simple gesture of solidarity, they become a source of hope and they have the potential to change people's lives. I am living proof."
Nestor Fantini, former political prisoner in Argentina

"People put up walls between each other—and it's largely down to ignorance or negative media portrayals. We fail to realize there are so many good things and so many good people in this world."
John Sato, World War Two veteran who took four buses to join an anti-racism march in Auckland after the March 2019 Christchurch shootings

---

"A political struggle that does not have women at the heart of it, above it, below it, and within it is no struggle at all."
Arundhati Roy, Indian author

"Let us remember: One book, one pen, one child,
and one teacher can change the world."
Malala Yousafzai, Pakistani education activist

———

"My government makes me angry. The police force
makes me angry. Homophobia makes me angry.
Luckily, anger is what motivates me."
Zhanar Sekerbayeva, an LBQ activist from Kazakhstan

———

"I never thought I'd be talking about police brutality
and standing up for human rights. You never know what
people are going through until it happens to you."
*Monicah Njoroge, Kenyan civil rights activist whose brother Evans
was murdered after taking part in a peaceful protest*

———

"Get up, stand up, stand up for your rights.
Get up, stand up, don't give up the fight."
Bob Marley, Jamaican singer

———

"Humanitarian work isn't criminal, nor is it heroic.
Helping others should be normal."
*Seán Binder, volunteer who was detained after provided
life-saving assistance to refugees in Greece*

———

Culled by Izunna Okafor